CONSCIOUS CONNECTION

CONSCIOUS CONNECTION

REFRAMING MENTAL HEALTH TO CREATE A THRIVING LIFE

SARAH WAYT

Copyright © 2019 Sarah Wayt
All rights reserved

Printed in the United States of America

Published by Author Academy Elite
P.O. Box 43, Powell, OH 43035
www.AuthorAcademyElite.com

All rights reserved. No part of this publication may be reproduced, stored in a retrieval system, or transmitted in any form or by any means for example, electronic, photocopy, recording without the prior written permission of the publisher. The only exception is brief quotations in printed reviews.

Eclipse artwork created by Freepix.

Paperback ISBN-978-1-64085-468-0
Hardcover ISBN-978-1-64085-469-7

Available in hardcover, softcover, e-book, and audiobook

Library of Congress Control Number: 2018960012

For Lola

My happiest thought
My deepest feeling
My truest belief

TABLE OF CONTENTS

Introduction ix

Section 1: Adventure

Chapter 1   Incarceration 3
Chapter 2   Limbo 23
Chapter 3   Aftermath 47

Section 2: Breakthrough

Chapter 4   Who are we? 57
Chapter 5   Programming. 63
Chapter 6   Who do we want to become? 69
Chapter 7   Genetic make up 75
Chapter 8   Quantum body 81
Chapter 9   Interconnected world. 87
Chapter 10 Breath of life 93
Chapter 11 Our gifts 99
Chapter 12 Understanding innocence 105
Chapter 13 Gratitude and forgiveness 111
Chapter 14 Who can we be? 117
Chapter 15 Walking with Power. 123

Section 3: Movement

Chapter 16　My daily check-up 131
　　　　　　　　Journaling 132
　　　　　　　　Bioenergetic exercise 132
　　　　　　　　Me time 133
　　　　　　　　Away from the comfort zone 134
　　　　　　　　Pushing the limits 135
Chapter 17　Adventure call 139

Appendix A:
CONSCIOUS CONNECTION
5-DAY TIMELINE CHALLENGE 143

Appendix B:
CONSCIOUS CONNECTION MOVEMENT 145

Acknowledgements 147

About Sarah Wayt 149

Endnotes 153

INTRODUCTION

We all experience some degree of hardship and trouble in our lives. It is something we come to expect as humans, and often it is the very thing that will inspire us towards great achievements. The stress we feel as part of those hardships and troubles is what motivates us to move forward and strive for a more harmonious existence. From waking up for work in the morning, when all we want to do is lay in bed for a few more minutes, to confronting a deeply held fear over sitting in the dentist's chair; stress is a necessary part of our experience if we are to make our way through life's never-ending minefield.

The great thing about being human is that we have the power of choice. We get to choose how we respond to the stress we are facing. The weighing of those choices is based largely on the perceived consequences of confronting, or not, the things that are stressing us out. If we choose to lie in bed and not get ready for work, we know the result would eventually be the loss of our job and the livelihood which keeps us living in the style we are accustomed to. If we choose to ignore the painful tooth and not seek the dentists' expertise, we know the decay will mean more pain and eventual loss of a much-needed incisor or molar. In short, we make our choices based upon the most preferred outcome for our future happiness.

What happens when the stress we experience far outweighs our power to make a choice? When the decision to respond healthily is stripped from our grasp and we are left helpless and unable to cope? During these terrible times, we enter a spiral of self-deprivation and despair that touches every part of our lives. It filters through our very existence changing everything we thought we knew about ourselves and the world in which we live. Our perception of safety shifts and leaves us grasping for a sense of understanding. We desperately reach for a feeling of normality which no longer seems to exist.

During extreme stress, we descend into the dark pit of mental illness where depression, anxiety, panic attacks, psychotic disorders, and post-traumatic stress disorders (PTSD)—to name but a few—lie in wait to drag us deeper into our personal despair. The walls of the pit begin to close in on us, and in the darkness, it feels as though there is no escape. Our reality becomes an endless battle of fighting to get through every day under the never-ending shadow of our tortured mind. We are desperate to be free of the torment, but succumb to a sense that there is no solace, only the inky blackness of enduring anguish.

Amidst the unending confusion, we experience a profound loss of self where we fail to recognise the person we are becoming compared to the person we once were. The culminating effect of the presenting stress and our inability to apply our usual coping mechanisms leaves us spiralling downwards as we try to cling on to some sense of sanity in our lives. At this point, we recognise that we need help. To claw our way back from the grasp of mental illness, we need a lifeline, a mental health torch that will guide us from the darkness back towards the light. Sometimes this torch will come from the medical profession, in whom we put our trust to fix the problems we are facing and get us back on the road to recovery. We effectively hand over what little power we have left to a professional in the hopes that they can be the light to guide us back to our healthy selves.

The medical profession is a wonderful institution ingrained into our lives as the problem solver for our health issues. If we

INTRODUCTION

have an injury, they are on hand to assess our wound and take the necessary steps to get us back on our feet and functioning optimally again. They are the go-to organisation for all our physical ailments. However, they are woefully ill-equipped when it comes to dealing with mental illness. They look at presenting symptoms and then begin a regime of *helpful* suggestions that usually encompass taking medications and seeking therapy. The medications offered serve to mask our symptoms and often carry side effects which can actually add to our sense of despair over time rather than alleviate it. Therapy sessions have us delve back into the cause of our problems by forcing us to face the stress again and again as a way to desensitise us to its overall effect. Neither of these approaches accounts for the variability between individual experiences, and we are offered a one-size-fits-all solution to get us back into our right mind.

One size doesn't fit all. We are unique individuals. We do, however, share fundamental commonalities as a species. These commonalities connect us at the deepest level of understanding ourselves and our place in the world. They show us a pathway to reclaiming the individual power to heal ourselves in times of crisis and to live a happy and functional life once more.

Abundant health and wellbeing are natural states we move away from when challenging circumstances come into our lives. We cannot increase or decrease our health and wellbeing as they are intrinsic constants. Sometimes, however, we require guidance in reconnecting with them at our core to regain the balance to live our lives with flowing abundance. I have worked with many groups and individuals seeking a greater understanding of how to overcome the problems they are facing. One of the first things I do in a consultation is take a full case history to build a timeline. This valuable tool gives me an overview of their condition. It shows me the progression from their inherent healthy state to the problem they are experiencing in the present moment.

In nearly all cases, there is a *maintaining cause*, a key element contributing to the problem. Let me give you a simple example. Someone shows up for a consultation with a chesty cough, which has worsened over time. I take a full case history and discover that for the past two years they have been sleeping in a bedroom that has rising damp. No matter how many homeopathic pills I give them, no matter how many reflexology or aromatherapy treatments they have, they will continue to suffer until they address the maintaining problem of the rising damp.

The same principle applies to mental illness, where maintaining causes are primarily made up of common emotional beliefs we attach to the experience we are having. Our beliefs are so strong they can fool us into a downward spiral of despair and rob us of any sense that at our core, we are beings of inherent health and wellness. Understanding the nature of these maintaining causes and working towards their elimination in our lives frees our body and our mind to be the creative beings we truly are to live a life of thriving health. I had been sharing this understanding with great success for over 20 years with my clients, and then in 2016, I was completely shaken off balance.

I had a personally traumatic experience that took my understanding of maintaining causes from theory to practice in my own life. I wobbled and became lost for a while as I bought into the deep attachment of my emotional beliefs and I suffered greatly as a result. I hit an incredible low which almost became my living reality—until I realised that this experience was actually a wonderful opportunity. I had been given a chance to practice and trust within myself everything I had been saying to others. I now look people in the eye and say with confidence, 'I know you have the power because I have healed myself.' I did it by practising the conscious connection methods I am sharing with you in this book.

INTRODUCTION

You are about to embark upon an adventure which gives you the opportunity to examine your maintaining causes and effectively rewrite your mental illness story. You are taken on a journey towards a deeper awareness of your own healing power by reframing your understanding of the experience you are having. By reading this book, you have chosen to begin the process of reclaiming your power and unlocking the healing wisdom that inherently resides within each and every one of us. The simple act of picking up this book and turning the pages is encouraging your mind to shine a light on a better pathway to understand the problems you are facing.

The first section of the book, 'Adventure', shares details of the events that led to my being given a diagnosis of PTSD and depression by the medical profession. It gives you an understanding of the extreme stress I faced and how it nearly took my life. I share my story as a valuable starting point in the adventure towards healing. Recording the events that led to my mental illness was a therapeutic process in itself as it gave me the opportunity to get it out of my mind, where it seemed so overwhelming, and into a timeline to reflect upon as I reconnected with my natural healing power. In this section, you are encouraged to begin looking at your painful experiences as a loving expression of the body's guidance system. Symptoms are viewed as friendly indicators to draw your attention to something that requires change within you to heal. In doing so, you begin to reframe the understanding of your mental illness as an internal adventure you can learn valuable lessons from.

In the second section, *Breakthrough,* we explore the pathway towards a better understanding of ourselves and our reactions to stress through the basic commonalities we share as human beings. We unpack emotional maintaining causes that have such a deep hold on how we see our situations and explore how we can begin viewing our troubles through different lenses. Each chapter gives details of beliefs we have held about ourselves and how we fit into the world around us. You are offered greater clarity of how to change those perceptions and regain your inherent healing power to move forward with natural energy flowing through your life.

In section three, *Movement,* I share how I applied a deeper understanding of my maintaining causes in everyday life to re-write my story. You will travel through a pathway that resonated deeply with my own healing as an example of what can be achieved, not as a template for you to follow. Your pathway to rewriting your mental illness story may take a very different form entirely. The key to finding your way lies in changing your perception of our commonly held beliefs and applying that insight to your own unique story in a way that resonates deeply for you. In doing so, you will be able to reclaim your individual power through greater self-awareness and turn your pain into a powerful torch which lights your way towards better mental health.

SECTION 1

Adventure

There is no greater agony than bearing
an untold story inside you.

—Maya Angelou[1]

1
INCARCERATION

Hi. I'm Sarah, and in 2016, as a 46-year-old woman, I was savagely beaten by my partner. I made my escape from where the abuse occurred and was put up by a friend in their house. I was in severe pain at the time, but I thought it would die down once the swelling and discolouration had gone. Little did I know, under the surface more serious problems were developing. After a few days, I was able to isolate areas of pain which seemed to be intensifying rather than subsiding—the pains in my stomach being one.

I'd always thought I had a high tolerance for pain, but after a few days of intense cramping and stitching it became apparent that whatever was going on was getting worse, and I needed help. By the time my friend called an ambulance, I was going into septic shock and unable to communicate.

I was rushed into the local hospital and given a scan which revealed my bowel had ruptured and I was dangerously close to death. The surgeons battled to save my life by removing my entire bowel and cleaning the abdominal cavity with litre upon litre of saline. The next thing I remember was waking up in the critical care unit after spending days in an induced coma. I had a wound from my solar plexus down to my pubic bone and a colostomy. Coming in and out of consciousness, I initially thought I was having a bad nightmare. My family was around me, and I should have begun to feel better; however, I remained in much pain I knew there was still something very wrong.

I was taken from critical care and placed on a general surgery ward to recover. The pains I had felt upon my arrival were still present but, as much as I insisted something wasn't right, everybody told me it was normal to experience pain after the laparotomy I had undergone. A week after my initial surgery, I was scanned again to find my concerns were justified. My spleen and my appendix had also ruptured, and I was bleeding out. I was rushed back into surgery and opened once again to have my spleen and appendix removed. Unfortunately, this time the surgeons were unable to close my stomach due to the amount of swelling from the two laparotomy procedures. I was left in critical care with an open wound covered by a vacuum-assisted closure (VAC) dressing which sucked away any built-up fluids, and I was told to prepare myself for an extended stay.

I was devastated. I'd had two lifesaving surgeries and now found myself back in critical care hooked up to machines by wires and tubes that seemed to come from everywhere. With my stomach wide open, I couldn't move, and being pumped full of Fentanyl, my spirits were low. It's true to say I began to feel overwhelmed by the condition I found myself in. The fallout from being attacked was taking its toll on not only my physical health, but my emotional/mental health as well. It was almost too much to comprehend that I would ever get over what was happening to me. I couldn't see the light at the end of this awful tunnel, and it seemed life had stopped as I knew it. I couldn't think anything about the future, only the now that was happening to me. I had no control, no say, and I'd found myself in a medical limbo which seemed never-ending.

I was told the first surgery carried a good six-week recovery period: a week in hospital, and four to six weeks at home. Now, as I had been opened up for the second time and my stomach hadn't been closed, terror began to grip me as to how long this would have to carry on. Lying in the critical care bed brought a fear like I'd never known. I was cared for on a one-to-one basis by a nurse who couldn't answer any of my questions. When the consultant arrived, all I could do in my drugged state was cry. My brain wanted to ask rational questions, but my ability to break through the fog of painkillers wouldn't allow me anything but tears.

Because I was falling in and out of coherence, it was difficult for me to keep track of who visited and what they had to say. I wanted to know what was going to happen. A family member informed me they had spoken to the consultant who had been quite evasive with any concrete information. Evidently, the procedures I'd had—if done individually—would have made for a sketchy recovery; combined, it meant a very slim chance of survival. Their philosophy at that point was to watch and wait to see if I would begin to recover. I remember sobbing and feeling completely helpless with a profound sense of vulnerability.

I didn't feel as though *I* as a person was important, but it was more like the condition I was in was a challenging puzzle to be solved. It was a powerless time for me, and I gave into this powerlessness by watching the hours tick by on the clock on the wall outside the nurses' station. Visitors came and went, filling me in on the details of their day as they chatted at me. I knew they were attempting to keep my mind occupied, but I couldn't quite grasp the thread of any conversations because their faces showed a depth of concern their lips didn't speak.

Kindly auxiliary nurses would smile and say hello as they went about their daily business. I would smile back but felt so removed from reality it was as though everyone was far away. They had a purpose in their daily tasks, and it felt as though my purpose had left me. Confined to a bed, I was unsure of what tomorrow would bring and if I would be alive to see it. I'd entered into a spiral of letting go and giving into the despair which seeped into my very bones.

Then the day came during the consultant's morning rounds where he unexpectedly turned to me and announced my vitals were nearing stability. I was by no means out of the woods, but he felt confident enough to move forward with closing up my stomach. He explained I would require a series of surgeries known as staged closures, where the surgical team would remove the VAC dressing under general anaesthesia, pulling my muscles and skin back into place a little at a time. There was uncertainty as to how many procedures this would take, but he felt confident the swelling in my stomach had lessened enough to begin, and my vitals were reaching a level that placed the surgeries within a safe threshold.

I have never known such terror as being wheeled down to the surgical centre to undergo the first closing procedure. In preparation for the event, I received a visit from the anaesthetist team who explained what would be happening during surgery. Their cheery disposition should have quelled any worries flying through my brain because, after all, they perform this every day of their lives. The previous two times of entering the surgical centre I had been mostly incoherent with pain and had no recollection of the process. Aside from my physical pain, I had also gone completely rigid with fear. My heart pounded so loudly I thought it would deafen me as I was wheeled from critical care through the endless corridors to my surgical destination.

Once seconded in the anaesthetists' room my anguish must have been clear from the tears that wouldn't stop falling from my frightened eyes. The team constantly reassured me everything would be fine; they would take great care of me, and it would all be over before I knew it. My shaking and palpitating heart begged to differ, but there was no way I could respond as I sank into the anaesthetic blackness.

Waking up in recovery after the first closure was harrowing. I woke screaming out in pain and had to be given 400mcg of Fentanyl on top of my daily allowance to calm me down and bring the pain under control before being released back to critical care. On the ward, I took a look at the closure, and it immediately dawned on me I would need many more surgeries as less than an inch of my stomach had come together. I sank to a depth of emotional torment with a feeling that I would never get out, I would never be better, and it would never end.

Through my intense distress, the pain began to grip me once more, and the ward doctor administered a shot of Ketamine. He assured me they would make progress quickly as they planned to take me back to surgery every three days to continue the closing. My heart sank again as I realised I would be stuck in this endless cycle of fear until it was done; then, as the Ketamine dose hit me, I didn't care. From that point on, Ketamine became part of my post-surgical regimen.

Six surgeries later, and regardless of knowing what to expect, my palpitations, tears, and shaking wouldn't stop. I was petrified and dreaded the surgical centre even though the staff had come to welcome me by name at that point. My stomach had been closed by around three inches, but there was so much farther to go. On the seventh surgery, we hit a complication. I woke up in recovery unable to breathe with a burning at my neck that felt like my head was ablaze. The recovery staff acted very quickly by opening my airway and trying to comfort me by bathing my neck with cool swabs. We later discovered that I had developed a sensitivity to Chlorhexidine, the antiseptic used in surgeries and in swabs to disinfect skin.

Stuck in a cycle of pain, fear, and brief Ketamine relief, the days and weeks that passed began to blur into an endless stream. I lost count of the number of surgeries I underwent to close the gaping hole in my stomach, my only reference point being the ever minutely shrinking VAC dressing I woke up with back in critical care. Then, one of the scariest and most inexplicable experiences to date happened.

I was taken down to the surgical centre for my next closure. The by now familiar dread and fear of what was to come had gripped me. The anaesthetic staff, well versed in my reaction to being there, carried out their usual hand-holding and reassuring stroking of my hair before putting me under. I expected to wake up in recovery and to be given extra Fentanyl to ease me a little before being taken back to critical care for a Ketamine shot; however, this time I didn't wake up in recovery—I woke up on the surgeon's table!

I woke with intense pain and a terrible tugging feeling in my stomach. The pain I was prepared for, but the tugging sensation was completely new and filled me with agonising fear. Something was terribly wrong. I could see the anaesthetist looking down at me, initially quite casually and then with a growing look of concern. He realised I was, in fact, awake and in my mind's eye I reached for his arm and screamed out for him to help me. In actual fact, my hand hadn't moved, and my screaming was deafening only in my head as no sound had escaped from my mouth. I was paralysed completely, and only my vital signs had given him any indication that I wasn't fully under anaesthetic. The tugging sensation I was experiencing was the surgical staff pulling my muscles and skin back into place. At that point, as I was enveloped by a silent scream, I delved once again into darkness.

As you can imagine, my usual levels of distress in recovery were heightened to the point of not being able to calm down regardless of how much Fentanyl I was given. I kept screaming, telling the surgical staff I'd woken up during the procedure, but nobody seemed to listen to me. It wasn't until I was back in critical care and had been given a few shots of Ketamine that I began to calm down a little. I was distraught but so drugged up at that point that I could only cry.

The ward doctors contacted the head anaesthetist who came and sat with me at my bedside. He couldn't apologise enough, saying that this situation should never have happened. He explained during staged closures, a lesser amount of anaesthetic is used compared to longer surgeries, I had obviously required more considering the number of surgeries I'd had previously. What I had experienced was referred to as anaesthetic awareness, a rare occurrence which he assured me wouldn't happen again.

From that point on my trust was completely gone, and I would beg and plead with the anaesthetic staff to make sure I wouldn't wake up while I was in surgery. My previous fears had now become heightened to almost a manic state, and I became dogged by panic attacks which culminated in screaming out for help, especially during sleep.

Almost a month had passed in critical care, and my stomach was now closed from my solar plexus down to my navel. My regular trips to the surgical centre carried the same psychological burden, and my despair at how slow the progress seemed dogged me every time I was brought back to the ward. I commented to some of the team about how dreary it was in critical care with no windows and how much I missed feeling the sun. They agreed this simple thing would probably help in my recovery and took me—bed and all—to a close by large side entrance one afternoon. It was a gloriously sunny May day, and I was overwhelmed by the breeze on my face and the birdsong coming from the trees across the road. After such a lengthy incarceration, I was so thankful for the fresh air and the warming sun that I couldn't speak; it felt as if I were experiencing real joy for the first time since the ordeal had begun.

The following afternoon, still basking from the glow of having gone outside, I was allowed to leave my bed and sit in one of the support chairs. With agreement from the physio that we could attempt a 15-minute break from lying down, the massive procedure of moving me began. I don't know why but the concept of having been stationary for over a month didn't enter my head until I attempted to stand. I had lain for so long the muscles in my legs wouldn't respond to my commands. It took all three nurses and the physio to get me to my feet and turn me on the plate to place me in the chair.

That evening there was a flurry of activity from the nursing staff, and a doctor was called to my bedside. I couldn't understand why there was a concern as I didn't feel any different than I had that morning. It transpired that the VAC dressing, which drained into a large container, was putting out an unusually coloured substance from my stomach. Tests revealed that I had sprung a leak from my friable bowel and the staged closures would have to stop until this new problem was remedied. I was once more thrown into a world of not knowing what would happen next, and any hope that I'd begun to build felt like it was slipping away bit by dripping bit.

I learnt over the next few days why my staged closures had been so slow. Having undergone 12 staged closures, my bowel had become friable, meaning it would take very little for it to begin to disintegrate. My bowel had responded by springing a leak, forming something called an entero-cutaneous fistula, an abnormal communication between the bowel and the skin. In short, I had a hole in a part of my intestine which was leaking fluid out through the VAC dressing into the container. At this point, the only clear action was to remove the VAC dressing completely as the suction would be sure to cause more damage to the intestinal hole. Great discussion then came into play as to how the fistula could be managed without the dressing. Effectively I had a large gaping hole from my navel down to my pubic bone, steadily seeping fluid, with little means of keeping it clean.

The medical staff tried all manner of different bags to affect a manageable solution, but the nature of the creases and curves in my lower abdomen made the task very difficult. Mostly the bags wouldn't stick due to abdominal liquid seeping into the adhesive, and I would find myself awash in corrosive internal fluid time after time. I began to feel like a baby having to have her nappy changed as there was no way I could manage to clean myself.

My hope had begun to wane with the knowledge there was no way I could have my stomach closed while this was going on. The light at the end of the tunnel got even darker when I was slapped with the next realisation from my consultant. To help the fistula heal, I had to rest my bowel completely. This meant I would no longer be able to eat or drink anything at all.

Just when I thought things couldn't get any worse!

At this point, I'd spent a little over a month in critical care, and regardless of having developed a fistula, I was reasonably stable, so the need for one-to-one nursing had passed. I was relieved when the decision was made to place me back onto the general surgery ward again. The surgical ward was a hubbub of noise and movement, a completely different feeling to the often-eerie stillness of critical care. It was here I got a true sense of how much danger I had been in. There were comments from different nurses who were glad to see me as they had not been told what happened after my rushed departure a month before. Many of them thought I hadn't made it from the desperate state I'd been in and were delighted to see they had been wrong.

My first morning on the ward brought the consultant's visit. He explained that, due to my nil-by-mouth status, they would have to place me on total parenteral nutrition (TPN) feed. TPN is a way of supplying all the nutritional needs of the body by bypassing the digestive system and dripping nutrient solution directly into a vein. This mechanism would ensure my bowel rested completely, giving the fistula time to heal in isolation. The surgical procedure had been scheduled for the afternoon, and I was reassured I didn't have to be worried as I would be required to stay awake during the whole thing.

Being wheeled down to surgery for the procedure, I was completely paralysed with fear. It felt as though something was gripping my heart and squeezing it harder and harder. By the time I arrived, I was hyperventilating with distress. A nurse came to collect me from the corridor. Her reassuring noises at the sight of my distress did nothing to calm me so she eventually went to get the surgeon who she hoped would assuage my fears by talking me through the procedure. My mind received the surgeon's message much as Charlie Brown heard his teacher in the cartoon classroom—as a series of 'wah wah wah' noises which were barely perceivable above the whooshing sound of my heartbeat swimming around in my head.

The procedure room was large and daunting. I was injected in the chest to numb the area where a tube would be fed into my subclavian vein. I was ordered to stay completely still, which is not easy when every single part of me was shaking with fear. I was also told I would be required to not breathe for a period of time while the tube was inserted and informed that this was the most important part of the procedure. I had been hyperventilating on my way to the room, and I genuinely didn't think I would manage to stay calm enough to comply.

Eventually, the ordeal was over, and I was taken back to my room in pieces over the whole episode.

A regular visitor was waiting for me in my room when I returned, and once the porter had left and the nurse had checked I was comfortable, I dissolved into uncontrollable tears. My visitor held my hand as I lamented that I wanted to leave, I wanted everything to be over with, and I wanted to get out of this terrifying place. I didn't think I could survive any more of it.

I've never been what I would class as a foodie. I'm not the type of person who would wake up in the morning, have breakfast, and then wonder what I could make for lunch, dinner etc. Food had never played a leading role in my life, and I looked upon the act of eating as a necessity rather than an enjoyment. I had even joked with friends in the past saying when there was a pill brought out that contained all the nutrients needed, rather than go through the rigmarole of having to think and prepare a meal, I would be a happy girl indeed. That all changed when I was nil by mouth.

There was no telling how long my bowel would need to rest; the consultant hoped the fistula would clear itself and couldn't give me a timeline of when this might happen. Each night I was hooked up to a feed bag via the TPN and unhooked in the morning so I could be free of the cumbersome tubing for the day. In the early days, it wasn't my not being able to eat that struck me; it was my not being able to drink anything, not even water.

Then the unexpected food cravings began. I had tasted the hospital food before the arrival of my fistula and—believe you me—it wasn't particularly appetising. The mind is a strange taskmaster when starved of oral stimulation. I would smell the food trolley arrive, and my brain would go off on a tangent about how delicious the coming meal must be—how juicy the meat, how tender the vegetables, how amazing the crispy potatoes would feel in my mouth. I found myself calling to the auxiliaries when they passed my door, asking them to relay to me what the options were regardless of my not being able to partake. Initially, they would be reluctant to share but eventually, they got used to my asking and would run through the delights of the day laughingly commenting I had gone completely mad.

At that point, I felt they might be right!

Over the weeks that followed, I had begun to get into a routine within the ward. It consisted of coming off my TPN every morning, getting myself out of bed, seeing my consultant, taking short slow walks down the corridor with the physiotherapist, and receiving visitors throughout the day. Every day was a struggle of trying to hold on to the hope this wouldn't be forever and the day would come when I would be able to leave.

My case file was taken care of by various departments within the hospital. My consultant was the one making all the major decisions, but he had also given my care over to the nutritionist, who was responsible for getting me adequate nutrients to survive. The physiotherapist was responsible for getting me back on my feet. The stoma nurses were responsible for the care of both stoma and fistula. The acute response team was responsible for checking the function of my feed line. And the pain management specialist was responsible for ensuring my pain was under control enough for me to move around. All my physical needs were being met. However, at no point were my psychological issues addressed.

My experiences up until this point—almost two months of hospitalisation—had left me with harrowing nightmares and periods of utter despair. My visitors were able to take me in a wheelchair to the sunny entrance doors as well as to the coffee house in the main building; however, even the sun couldn't lift me on my down days. I knew the whole situation had obviously taken its toll on me, but I couldn't understand how one day I could feel emotionally well whereas the majority of my time was spent silently despairing and sobbing alone. I wanted more *well* days, and having visitors saying 'Well, you have been through an awful lot' didn't help me overcome the bleak darkness growing inside.

Some days I recognised triggers that would drag me down. If I'd woken after a night of terrifying dreams, if I was having a particularly hard time with the fistula seeping through and covering me with faecal matter, or if I was craving for a cup of tea, I would plummet into a desperate spiral of self-pity I couldn't lift myself from. Then, other times there would be no trigger. I would sit and feel so incredibly unhappy tears wouldn't stop falling, and no matter how many reassuring words were spoken to me, I couldn't lift myself out of the dark place I occupied. I kept putting conditions on my happiness: When I'm able to eat again I will feel happier; when I can walk to the end of the ward corridor I will feel happier; when the fistula stops pumping its corrosive fluid out of my stomach I will feel happier. All these thoughts served to do was keep me in a spiral of wanting change and then feeling desperate when it didn't happen.

After six weeks of being nil by mouth and relying on the TPN feed to sustain me, the fistula still hadn't shown any signs of letting up. The daily measurements of fluid it excreted had remained around 100mls for about a week, and the decision was taken to allow me to begin manually taking in fluids and small amounts of food each day. The idea was to watch and see how the fistula responded. If the output increased significantly, I would have to return to the TPN; if not, I could return to reasonably normal eating while the fistula was monitored. It was time to test one of my conditions of happiness and see if the darkness would begin to lift.

So, the decision was made; I could eat and drink again. I think the staff on the ward were almost as excited as I was when the nil by mouth sign was wiped off the board on my wall. There were rules that I had to abide by if I were to keep the fistula output under control, and my nutritionist laid them out for me over our next hour's discussion. I would begin with soups to ease my body back into eating, but I would have to avoid fibre completely as it is one of the hardest things for the stomach to process. She began to reel off a list of food items I could not indulge in and immediately my heart sank. Yes, you guessed it, all my favourite foods were banned! No nuts, seeds, cereals, fruits, or vegetables were allowed with only a few exceptions. I could have potato, but the skin was strictly forbidden, so only mash or boiled was permitted. I was allowed to eat bananas, as the skins were removed but that was my only fruit. Aside from that, I could eat cheese, eggs, meats, and fish with no coating; I was to chew everything until it was mush in my mouth before swallowing to make it easier for my stomach to digest.

The days that followed were a tentative exploration of what and how much I could eat coupled with paranoia over what, and how much would come out of the fistula. When I had been on the TPN feed, everything that fell out of the hole in my stomach had been in liquid form: a brownish green flow which would collect in the bag ready for measuring. Once food was re-introduced, this liquid became much thicker, more like slurry which would accumulate on the surface of my skin making it much more difficult to keep clean.

I had entered my seventh week of being on the surgical ward without the VAC dressing, and the gaping hole I once had was beginning to heal out to form a deep crater. The endless annoyance of having the bag leak was an ongoing problem, but the worst part was my not being able to change and clean it myself. I had mastered the art of cleaning and changing my colostomy bag, but the fistula hole was positioned further down towards my pubic area and, with the muscles of my stomach not being in place, I couldn't move my head to see it.

On one occasion, while waiting on nursing staff who were busy attending others, the stoma nurse walked into my room and found me desperately clasping swabs to the area to stem the 'slurry' flow. She took over and cleaned the area ready to receive a new bag. I explained to her my frustrations over having to wait each time for someone to help me, and she came up with the idea of giving me a mirror so I could attempt the change myself. We played around for a while with the positioning of the mirror on my over-bed table and eventually got it in the right place so I could see what was going on. This was the first time I had actually been able to see the fistula for myself; it looked horrendous like a deep red sinkhole with an opening at the centre about an inch long.

With her help, I managed to get the new bag positioned and stick it down with flange supports for extra grip. It had taken a while, and I was sore from craning to see properly in the mirror, but I had done it. It took a few more times of leaks and changes to master the art, but master it I did. One more step in the right direction towards independence!

Step by little step I was beginning to recover. From being unable to move, I was now taking very slow steps towards the end of the ward corridor. From being unable to eat, I was now enjoying a limited variety of food and drinks. From being unable to clean and change my bags, I was now becoming quite adept with my trusty mirror. It was time to begin asking the questions that were uppermost in my mind. When would I be taken to surgery to have the fistula mended and my stomach closed fully? And, eventually, when would I be allowed to leave?

I had now been hospitalised for nearly three months. My vitals were only taken three times a day and not at night (compared to the checks every two hours when I had arrived on the ward), and I was managing to do everything by myself without the aid of nurses. I decided now was the time to ask my consultant about how he intended to proceed with a plan to fix the fistula. It was a painful discussion to have; he began by explaining that having had so many surgeries in such a short space of time meant there was no way they would be able to open me up again. My bowel had become so friable that even trying to find where the leak was coming from meant permanent loss of function.

I was incredulous; they couldn't intend for me to have a leaking stomach for the rest of my life. Surely not! He assured me no, there was no intention of leaving me like this permanently, because he still hoped the fistula would clear on its own. He also pointed out the recovery periods for the procedures I'd already had—three months for each laparotomy and about a month for each staged closure. Counting up in my head, I realised it would be over a year and a half before he would consider any further movement forward. I had become accustomed to feeling devastated at this point, but the news still crushed me into silence for the remainder of the day.

The following day I began making plans about how I would deal with the news I'd received. When the consultant appeared on his morning rounds, I decided to tell him I intended to leave the hospital. I told him my recovery would be better served if I were in my own space rather than tethered to the hospital. He wasn't happy; he had intended for me to remain in hospital under observation for as long as possible and didn't think it would be good for me to go. I bit the bullet and politely told him either he would agree with my release date, or I would check out under my own steam. He reluctantly agreed, with certain stipulations:

1. I would have to have a doctor for prescriptions
2. I would have to have a fixed abode to be released to

At this point, I realised I had neither of the above and would have to start preparing them as soon as possible if my plan was to come to fruition. As soon as he left my room, I rang the local doctors' surgery. They informed me to register with them meant coming down to the surgery and filling in forms. I got myself dressed in outside clothes and made my way, very slowly, to the elevator at the end of the ward and down to the reception area where I phoned for a taxi to collect me.

I was exhausted when I got in the taxi; the descent from the ward had taken all my energy, but I wasn't deterred from the matter at hand. A short journey later and I made my way to the doctors' counter for the forms, and then to a nearby chair to fill them in. It was a bizarre feeling being out in public again. My heart was racing, and I began to feel really uneasy. My stomach was screaming from the exertion, and I felt sick and lightheaded as I tried to concentrate on the forms in front of me. My focus became very abstract, as if I were seeing through water, and then I realised I was crying. I had a tingling, almost buzzing, feeling in my toes and fingers, with a tightness to my chest that made me feel as though I would wretch. I couldn't see the forms, let alone fill them in, and became so overwhelmed by the sounds and lights around me I thought I would pass out. I wanted to escape, but my stomach wouldn't allow me any movement without excruciating pain. All I could do was sit and shake uncontrollably.

I must have sat like that for around half an hour when the receptionist came over to me to ask if I was okay. I couldn't speak. A tight lump had formed in my throat, and no matter how hard I tried, I couldn't force any words out. She went to a dispenser and placed a cup of cold water into my trembling hands saying, 'It's okay. Breathe.' I hadn't realised I was suffering from a panic attack and hadn't been able to catch my breath properly. She had recognised the symptoms straight away and sat with me while I calmed down enough to fill in the forms.

I had sorted out who would be my doctor, albeit painfully! Now I had to sort out where I would live. As you are aware, I had escaped from a domestic abuse situation to my friend's house, and although I was welcome to return there, I knew to move on truly was to move forward towards my own place. I didn't have a clue where I would start, and sitting in my hospital bed, I was quite contemplative about first steps. A cleaning orderly suggested I contact the domestic abuse team with the local council who would be able to point me in the right direction. That afternoon, while sitting outside in the sun, I made the call.

A lovely man answered the phone, and I stammered for the words to explain my situation. He was very patient and allowed me the time to gather myself together and begin my story. I told him I had been abused, in hospital for nearly four months, and couldn't be released unless I had somewhere to go. That was about all I could manage before the realisation of what I'd been through burst out of me as a flood of uncontrollable tears. He quickly took my phone number and assured me he would call me back with information of services I could access. I sat there and felt numb with the pain of it all, feeling the huge despair of what I'd told him. It seemed so unreal and so painful at the same time. Acknowledging this had happened to me was the heaviest feeling I had ever experienced, and it felt as if I might sink under the weight of it all.

INCARCERATION

Later I received a call back telling me there were steps I must take to ensure the smooth transition from hospital to a woman's refuge which was to be my safe haven. Relief washed over me as I realised I had fulfilled the consultant's second requirement for my release within a few days. After four months hospitalisation, armed with an outpatients' appointment, my prescription, and my meagre belongings, the day finally arrived where I was to leave and begin to take care of myself again.

This chapter shows the very beginning of my descent into mental distress. Physically being unable to move after my first surgery brought intense feelings of fear, which echoed through my entire hospital stay. The helplessness I felt took hold of me mentally and fed by the emotion of fear, began to shape the remainder of my experiences. It is clear to see how day after day this fear grew exponentially and in doing so altered my perception of safety. I could feel my mental health beginning to slip away when I knew something else was wrong after my first procedure. Having those fears ignored left me feeling even more disempowered by the professionals who wouldn't listen to my justified concerns. The subsequent complications during my stay intensified my helpless feelings, leaving me with a sense that I had no control over my healing.

Anything that could go wrong did go wrong, and it seemed my body was letting me down at every turn. This increased my anxiety and contributed to developing PTSD and panic attacks. Helplessness was the first step towards developing a stress response of frightening nightmares, which began to haunt my sleep, and anxiety, which hit me daily. Extreme fear left an imprint upon my soul which translated into the panic attack I suffered when I attended the doctor's surgery. The culmination of this harrowing time brought vulnerability into my life which intensified over the following weeks and months.

2
LIMBO

Saying goodbye to the staff at hospital was a mixed bag of fear that I would be out in the world alone now, and gratitude for all they had done for me. Travelling in my sister's car to the woman's refuge, I wondered what this new move would mean for me. I had never been in the situation of refuge housing before and wasn't sure what to expect. We pulled up outside and were welcomed by a jolly woman—Elaine—at the door. She had kind, smiling eyes and I was immediately relieved and felt safe as we were taken into the lounge on the ground floor.

I was given a cup of tea, and the induction process began. The financial assistance I had requested while at hospital had been granted and all bills for staying at the shelter were covered. All I would need to supply for myself was food. It felt like being in a boarding school, but in my condition, the rules weren't difficult to follow, and I readily filled in and signed the agreement sheets, grateful to know I had a roof over my head.

After the induction, Elaine took us on a tour of the house, and I was finally shown to my room, a large airy space with everything I could possibly need to make my stay comfortable. My sister left me to settle in, and I locked my door, put on the kettle to make the first drink I'd made in four months, and sank into a chair. My first night at the refuge consisted of tossing and turning to get comfortable with the bags, which constantly got in my way. When I did find sleep, I woke many times drenched in sweat from terrible dreams of screaming out in pain and terror. By the time morning arrived, I was drained and exhausted from the night's ordeal. In the days that followed, I stuck to my own company, barely leaving my room.

I knew to keep up with my recovery meant I needed to take short walks and build my strength, but in my present state all I could do was sit and stare out of my window. Elaine suggested I come to the office and get the ball rolling on house hunting as a way to lift my spirits. We went online and filled in the forms required to get me started, and with this done I went into the garden to get the first sunshine and fresh air I'd had in three days.

Over the next month, it became apparent all was not calm in the house. Tensions escalated as personalities clashed between the other residents, and this culminated in a house meeting where tempers became inflamed. I found the whole experience harrowing as indignant denials flew and a full-scale squabble filled the space. I went to see Elaine after the meeting had broken up and voiced how difficult I had found the confrontation. While it had been happening, my heart had started to pound in my ears, and I recognised the beginnings of a panic attack from the level of anger and frustration that had circled in the room.

I explained to Elaine that if I couldn't feel safe in the space, I wouldn't be able to stay. She understood completely and suggested, as I hadn't been successful in finding a suitable council flat, maybe I should begin to look at privately-rented homes as a way to expedite the process.

Over the next few weeks, my daughter and I viewed many private flats and finally found one suitable for our needs. It was on the ground floor, close to a local park with a small string of shops to the end of the street, and ready to move into immediately. We filled in the paperwork, paid the deposit, and made the arrangements for a moving date. As much as I was grateful to the refuge for providing me with a roof over my head, I was more grateful to be leaving it, and the squabbling residents, behind.

The morning I picked up the keys to my new home was a very happy occasion indeed. There is nothing quite like having a front door that can be locked and a safe space that belongs to you. Having spent so long in the care of others with no control over who came and went, it was a breath of fresh air to finally have something I could call my own again.

The thought of ordering new furniture passed through my mind, but it seemed so silly considering I still had a house full of my belongings. My mind was made up. I would contact my abuser and arrange to collect my stuff as soon as I could. I also decided, as I was taking such a big step, now would be the time to report the abuse to the police as a safeguard should my ex become a problem.

The thought of going through the abuse bit-by-bit with the police hit me hard. I spent days wondering if I would be able to get through it all without breaking down and concluded that I wasn't strong enough. The only thing I could think of doing was writing the account down so that I didn't leave anything out, and I began the long process of recording the ugly incident on paper. I was both relieved and traumatised once it was complete. I couldn't quite believe it had happened to me and felt sick to my painful stomach at the horror I had endured. I then contacted my ex and told him I would be coming to collect my belongings within the month, requesting he give me five days of peace to pack and be on my way. He was surprisingly cordial and agreed to my request, saying he would find somewhere to stay and leave me in peace while I was back in the house.

CONSCIOUS CONNECTION

The day of retracing the journey back to my old house was looming, and aside from my usual night terrors, my sleep became a pattern of endless scenarios flying around my head. I would go to bed and lie there for hours fretting about how it would feel returning to the scene of the crime. How would I manage to pack up an entire house in my delicate state? How would I report the abuse and much more besides? Of course, I couldn't know the answers to any of these thoughts, but my mind wouldn't let go, and when the day finally arrived, I was a complete mess.

When we arrived and were settled, my sister and I went to the local police station and asked to speak to someone. My decision to write the whole thing down proved to be right as I couldn't find the words to speak when sitting in the small room. Later that day, a man came to the hotel and requested a form signed to gain access to my medical records. He informed me that, due to the seriousness of the crime, I had been passed on to the Criminal Investigation Department (CID). He gave me the details of the officer in charge and told me to call if I experienced any problems with the move. The next morning, we went to my house to begin packing up, and it quickly became apparent I would need to use these details.

Every day we were in the house my ex would text me. When I received the first text, I was distraught and immediately contacted CID to ask for guidance. They told me under no circumstance should I open the door to allow him in the house. If he did approach, I must dial 999 to ask for immediate assistance, quoting the case number he had issued me with. I replied to the text by telling my ex the instructions I'd received. He was undeterred, and each day I would receive another text requesting admittance. I became so unnerved at the thought of him arriving I asked the removals firm if we could possibly bring the date forward due to the circumstances. They agreed, and on the morning of the fourth day, we were packed and ready to get on the road.

Back in my little flat, I was completely exhausted and in considerable pain. The removals men were absolute angels and placed all the heavy furniture where it would live, leaving me with a sea of boxes to unpack at my leisure. I was now home surrounded by boxes of my stuff, and I broke down completely. I don't know if it was sheer relief that I had closed the door to my past with my ex or sheer joy to have my belongings around me once more, but I spent the evening on my sofa sobbing uncontrollably. I made a pledge to myself I would tackle a box a day until it was done but with my physical restrictions, I didn't have the energy to do it. Some days I would slump onto my sofa in absolute agony thinking I would never get through it all as the pains in my stomach worsened.

I noticed during a change of the fistula bag that my abdominal hole had decreased so much there was only a very small opening. I had thought the extra pain I experienced was due to my increased activity. However, it began to dawn on me that the skin that was trying to heal was rubbing together every time I moved. The crater edges were as large as they had been in hospital, and the skin was so red it looked as if it had bleed lines running through it. Cleaning the area, I would have to grit my teeth until the task was done and then apply the bag, making sure not to stick it to the sore skin. It was becoming difficult to manage, and I laid off unpacking for a while to give it a rest.

I stuck to the hospital regime of not digesting any fibre in my diet; however, I noticed regardless of my food intake, eating had begun to have a worse effect on the fistula, causing me a lot of discomfort when it was leaking. Where the skin had come closer together, the slurry after every meal would have to push its way through the small hole to escape into the bag. This pushing through would begin around 20 minutes after digesting anything and caused me to bend over clinging to furniture until the pain passed. It was time to make a visit to the stoma nurses when I attended my first consultants' outpatient appointment to see what could be done.

As the taxi brought me closer to the hospital entrance for my first outpatient appointment, I felt a tightening in my chest and a buzzing in my head. I was shaking so much that when I handed over the taxi fare, I almost dropped the money. I was 20 minutes early for my appointment, so I decided to make my way to the coffee shop in the main building to try to calm my nerves. I had understood it might be stressful to return to the hospital, but I wasn't prepared for the fear and panic descending upon me.

Sitting in the outpatient waiting area, sipping my hot drink, I found it nigh on impossible to calm down. By now I had developed a pain in my chest, and I couldn't catch my breath. Every sip of my coffee became a chore to swallow as it felt like a lump had formed in my throat. All I wanted to do was to escape and run away back to the safety of my home. Eventually, I was called in to see the consultant, but the pesky lump in my throat stopped me from speaking, and I sat in the chair shaking my head with tears in my eyes. He popped me onto the couch and began taking off my fistula bag to see how it looked. All I could do was shake or nod my head as he examined me. He said, 'The fistula looks very sore. It must be causing you quite a lot of pain. Are you still managing to eat?'

He placed me back into the waiting area to see the stoma nurse. I intended to stay there as instructed, but after five minutes my heart was pounding so hard I couldn't catch my breath. I needed fresh air, I needed to get out, I needed to get away, and before I knew it I had risen from my seat and made my way outside. As the fresh air hit me, I thought I would be sick. I gasped for it to fill my lungs and sank down onto a bench by the entrance. If I could sit there for a minute, maybe I would calm down. But the thought of walking back into the hospital filled me with dread, so I called a taxi and made my way back home.

Three days later, I received a package through the post of anaesthetic cream with a note from the stoma nurse. I lay down, took off my bag, and slathered the cream all over the crater in my stomach. Relief, albeit brief, flooded through me as the cream began to take effect. After revelling in the pain-free moment, I put on my new bag, clamped it in place with flange supports, and stood up. Within minutes, the bag was making its way to the floor. The cream was so greasy it had slipped right off!

Over the weeks that followed, I spent hours lying on the sofa with my bag off and the anaesthetic cream in place. I couldn't apply a bag to the area with the cream on, so I lay like that to gain some relief from the persistent pain. It was becoming difficult to move around the house, let alone go for my daily walk, so I began to spend more and more time indoors.

I love to read, but with painkillers coursing through my system I found it difficult to concentrate for long periods of time. I would find myself re-reading passages from my book, frustrated I couldn't retain the information I had just read. I picked up jigsaw puzzles I'd had for ages and never done. Again, my concentration was so scattered I would end up staring at the pieces rather than putting them into the desired order.

I had friends pop round to the house to try to rouse my spirits, but I would find I couldn't fully engage with conversations, and my mind would wander into self-pity. A friend who had become a regular visitor found my absences quite frustrating, and one afternoon informed me it seemed like I had become so consumed by my pain that our friendship wasn't important anymore. I was exhausted and knew everything else seemed insignificant compared to the scorching heat of the volcanic liquid as it made its way onto my sore skin, but I hadn't expected this statement from my friend.

I went into a spiral of worry and fear. Did all my friends feel this way? Was everyone finding me difficult to be around? Was I becoming a burden? It was at that point I began to shrink back from people, family included. I decided they must all have much better things to do than be around someone like me and I would cry off when asked for a visit, making excuses I was in too much pain.

I couldn't find any joy in my life. Days became a spiral of waking in sweats from terrors during the night, dragging my tortured body from the bed onto the sofa, and then dragging it back every evening to begin another uncomfortable attempt at sleep. Most days I took to lying bagless for as long as my bladder could hold out, and then when I could hold on no more, I would re-bag and make my way to the bathroom. I began to eat less and less, preferring to avoid the painful evacuations as much as possible. The stoma nurse would screw her face up in sympathetic pain when seeing me at her clinic. She could see from the red raw colour of the skin how much I was suffering. Where the crater had continued to try to heal, its efforts had begun to cause the skin to pucker into deep rivulets. These deep folds were impossible to pull apart to clean and had, therefore, become spaces to catch faecal matter, allowing it to fester on my already raw skin.

The nurse explained that the skin's healing action had caused over-granulation, leaving the tissues excoriated. In short, my skin was continuing to grow and was forming deep, painful lesions since I was unable to keep it clean. She suggested I go to see the consultant at the hospital again. The thought of enduring another appointment struck me full blow in the chest. I asked if there was anything he would suggest that she couldn't. She stood pensive for a moment and shook her head sadly. Hating the pained look she had adopted, I immediately felt really sad for her and told her not to bother the consultant. If there was nothing they could do, I would painfully continue as I had and not bother them again until it was time for my next scheduled hospital appointment in three months. She gave me some Lignocaine patches and gel to help with the pain, and I made my way back home feeling overwhelmingly dejected.

Having exhausted all avenues of treatment and unable to get much joy from the medical profession, I took the only course of action I could think of and stopped eating altogether. My reasoning being that if I didn't put very much in, I wouldn't have pain when it was coming out. This mostly worked with my only consuming fruit tea and honey. The pain was still there, the skin was still incredibly sore, but I wasn't making it worse with food that made the excretions so thick and glue-like to my skin. I was due for my next appointment with the consultant towards the end of April, so I had been living the fistula nightmare for nearly a year. I could no longer walk comfortably, and the pain from my fistula had been met with multiple hernias which began popping through the separated abdominal wall.

My next appointment turned into another hospital stay when my consultant realised I had stopped eating. My heart sank into my boots; I was to be brought back to the place I was so terrified of. The idea was to force me to eat food while I was on the ward for the pain management team to see the effect it had on me when it came out of my stomach.

I obediently ate the dinner they provided and waited for the inevitable agonising ejection of it through the fistula.

Witnessing my distress, the pain nurse immediately called for Oxycodone, administered in 5ml liquid form every hour until the pain subsided. She also placed me initially on a low dose of Pregabalin capsules, leading up to 600mg a day, in the hopes it would help with the nerve pains around the fistula.

I had to stay on the ward for five days while they assessed my pain levels. They didn't force me to eat after the first day but did insist I take Fortijuce and PEPTAMEN drinks daily, which would provide me with all the nutrients I needed. I grew quite sullen in my incarceration, so I quietly agreed and was allowed to return home under my new drink regime. The following six months were filled with consistent pain and anguish over my condition. There seemed to be no escape as I plunged into desperate darkness. The following diary extracts show how far down my pain took me.

Excerpt from my May 2017 diary:

This is a nightmare, a recurrent brain splitting and soul-destroying nightmare.

I don't know how long I can hold on.

Every day becomes the same endless painful struggle of trying to sit up in my bed while I have no integrity to my stomach. The wrench I feel from the lack of musculature is second only to the splintering pain of the open wound upon bending in two to stand.

The sickening dribble of caustic fluid from the fistula filters its way down over my pubic bone into the bag where it has been collecting during my torturous sleep. To take one step away from the bed fills me with sickening pain as I hold my stomach to try to regain balance.

One step ... and then another, and another, as I become more accustomed to the awful reality that I have survived another day, I have to live through another day ... another pain filled day.

The real splitting pain is coupled with a soulful sob, and I don't know if they can be separated now—the pain in this wretched body and the pain in my soul.

Sobs release with each step and they deepen as I look at my disgusting shape in the full-length mirror. The disfigured mess, misshapen from the cutting of my flesh by the surgeons—from the countless hernias where my muscles have lost their memory of where to be. The chaos of healing that comes after the butchery of operation after operation. The deepest sob and a wrench of pain as I reach up to gather my dressing gown from the door to close the curtain on this dismal disgusting mess.

So, I have to live through another day. I have to persevere through this pain again. I have to witness what a mess I am once more. I don't want to. I don't want this. I don't have the strength to push myself when there is no more endurance left.

But slowly, very slowly, I make my way from my room. One painful step at a time towards the bathroom. Counting the steps through the lounge to take my mind off the wrenching agony in my stomach. Through the kitchen and finally into the bathroom.

I stand, like a man, in front of the toilet, looking at the thick brown slurry sitting in my bag. I have to take my hands away from supporting my abdomen as I bend down to capture the toilet paper by the side of the bowl; I stifle my sobs as the pain rips through me. I have to empty the bag. It takes two hands, so I can't try to stop the pain by holding my belly; I must endure the stinging torture for a while longer as I pull at the Velcro holding the bag tightly shut. At last, it's free, but now I must stand and wait as the thick brown sludge makes its way slowly from the bag down to the toilet bowl. It seems to take an endless time as gloopy slurry falls from the pouch.

At last, it is done; at last, the bag is empty, and I can sit, clutching my stomach as the welcome release of my bladder distracts me. Knowing that once I'm done, I will once again have to go through the torment of standing up.

I take a second to muse back to a simpler time—a time when waking up was more like a dream of sleepily stumbling out of my bed, half comatose waddling through the house, having a pee, and staring through blurry eyes at the tired face looking back at me in the mirror. Now, as I pull myself to my feet, I am agonisingly aware that I am awake as every nerve in my body screams to attention at the effort of it all.

I no longer like to look in the mirror to see the lines of fatigue etched across my face—a face that has seen so much torture at the hands of a madman as well as the hands of the surgeons in the hospital. It's like looking at a stranger now. The eyes are the windows to the soul, and mine hold the image of a woman that is lost, so very lost, and so incredibly alone. It's conceited to think nobody knows the trouble I feel, but I feel so alone with the pain I endure as I walk with this torment and tragedy.

The daily grind begins with feeding my beautiful cats, Leo, my ginger tom; and Poppy, my black queen. They are great joys in my life, but even they have become a trial of endurance. Their food sits in a plastic bucket in the kitchen, and to bend down to pick up the food bag as well as their bowls always proves to be a challenge. Even more of a challenge when Leo insists on walking away from his food with his nose held high like I've placed something foul before him. I find myself cursing him as I bend down once more to save his food from the gluttonous Poppy and put it up on the side for him for later.

And then, whatever the weather, the back door is opened and they both skip out to sample the morning air. Leo and Poppy move so easily, so incredibly lithe like, and my mind returns to a time when I was likened to a cat with my feline moves and reflexes. If I weren't in so much pain, I would laugh at the total contradiction to now, but to laugh causes me so much agony. Not that there's much to laugh about anymore.

Standing causes less pain once I'm up, so I take the opportunity to fill the kettle and get my cup ready for tea to take my morning pills. I've gone from a girl that never took any medications to someone that will have to take them for the rest of her life. I feel like a traitor to myself, like I've let myself down. I have to admit to needing the painkillers, after all ... what kind of mess would I be without them? I keep telling myself it's not forever, it will come to an end when my fistula and hernias are dealt with, and then I will be able to begin the process of weaning myself away from such heavy killers.

The popping of the kettle draws my mind back to the present, and I fill my cup with my favourite amber liquid. My cup of tea is a far cry from what I would like to be tucking into. Again, I am left to muse on times gone by when I would hungrily tuck into a bowl of fruit topped with granola and yoghurt, or a full English breakfast of sausage, bacon, eggs, mushroom, tomatoes, and baked beans. Now, food is like a distant memory, one which makes me sigh knowing I can live without it but would dearly like to have it in my life.

I can eat; it's not like my mouth has been sewn shut or anything, but I can't eat without suffering terrible pain. It feels like red hot lava over broken skin. Like cut glass being pushed into my stomach in a constant, never-ending nightmare which takes my breath from my body and has me doubled over in agony. The only way to ease the pain is to hold on to my stomach, however, when I do it's like pushing the glass in further. It's white-hot rather than red-hot. It has gotten worse over the time I have been like this.

It started off like red-hot ants moving over the skin at the wound. They would constantly be moving and causing me great discomfort. Then, as time moved on, it became worse and worse. Too painful to handle, it's a pain the rips down through my belly into my very soul and has me screaming out for it to stop. When it doesn't, I'm left in a foetal position sobbing deeply at the longevity *of it. So, for now, I'm stuck with my cup of tea knowing I have to bend in pain again just to sit on the sofa.*

I feel wretched; I feel so unhappy and completely desolate that there is nothing I can do about it.

I want to feel better, and I've tried everything in my holistic repertoire to make it so.

Breathing into my space should settle me; it should at least afford some sense of distraction, but it doesn't. I can't seem to calm my senses to ground myself let alone to heal myself.

The pain pushes through me like waves, and the only thing I can do is to go with them. There is no pushing it into a box, a cloud, a void, and letting it float away on the wind. As I try, the next wave jolts through me like a sickening reminder I still have to live with this hell.

What is it all for? What is it preparing me for? Why do I have to keep reliving this nightmare day after day? Could I have been so wicked that I deserve eternal torture? Will this ever stop?

Questions … always questions flooding my mind and torturing my soul.

Why me? Why can't I heal? What is this all for? How can it end?

Every day these same questions come flooding into my mind, and there are never answers; there is never any inkling of what is happening and why.

I crave sweet dreams—dreams of sunny days looking out at a calm sea with the birds soaring high above my head and the warm breeze on my face.

I hear whispers through the trees and the carry of the ancestors' voices as they tell me the secrets of old. It is a comforting dream I haven't had in so long.

Instead, I am confronted with a darkness from which frightening faces with raging anger fly at me, taunting me, and laughing at the pain I'm in like they're torturing my soul.

There is no solace in the darkness; there is only fear. It is a cold, consuming fear which freezes my heart and has me waking screaming in a cold sweat.

There is no release from these terrifying dreams, as night after night they haunt me, following me into my slumber, and clawing at me until I am awake, only to find me again once I close my eyes.

You would think that I would be relieved in the morning when the dreams have left me, but the pain of waking up makes the torture of sleep seem like child's play.

And here I am sitting on my sofa, wishing it would all end, wishing it would all go away. Stop. Cease. Desist.

Every day is misery—being trapped, feeling the torment, fighting the pain, and then waking up to do it all over again. Feeling so alone, so in pain, and not able to share it with anyone.

My life is a pity party for one which relives itself over and over again like a really crappy soap opera continuing episode after episode, season after season. Trapped in a cycle of crap that is never-ending, I'm fighting not to be consumed by the torment of it all, but when every day is the same spiral down into the dark abyss, fighting feels so pointless.

I look back on my life now and it's hard to grasp the happy memories amidst the painful ones. It might be because of the darkness I feel now and how consuming it is. I'm grasping to feel the good; I'm seeking the happiness.

How do I find purpose again? How do I work out my life while I'm like this? There are inspirational quotes all over the house, but I feel nothing when I read them. They are nice, but they're not feeling for me. I can't see anything. I can't see my career. I can't see my life. I can't see a damn thing. I can't escape the nightmare. Maybe I should have died in the hospital, maybe I shouldn't have cheated death, or maybe I shouldn't have survived. It's another nightmare which drags me into the horrible place once again. Tears begin to flow, and I'm right back to staring into the abyss and wondering what I'm supposed to do.

I don't know how I'm going on. I don't know how I'm living each day with this pain, but somehow, I am. Somehow the dirge that is every day unfolds and I'm still here at the end of it. I can't ignore the pain and concentrate on anything else. Every time I try, my soul crushes in on itself, and I'm back to the pain again.

If I die, the pain will be gone, and I will be able to begin the next great adventure.

This is hard; it's the hardest thing I have ever had to do in my whole life. I'm resisting the urge to let the peace in and allowing myself to drift off and away on a tide of painless peace. Falling into a blissful sleep which takes me back to the ancestors. Back to the old knowledge. Back to the arms of everything that was, everything that is, and everything that is to come.

I tell myself that life doesn't have to stop after I die. It goes on. There is more; the next adventure is unknown, but it's there. The death of the body doesn't mean the energy is gone. Energy can't die. It's one of the things science has proven. Energy is there, around us, and working through us all the time. Once my body has taken its last breath my energy will be free— free of pain and free of everything that ties me to this wretched body.

The only way to get through this is to listen to my inner voice which tells me that I am strong enough every single day. Even when I don't believe it in the moment, I have to tell myself I can do this. I can take everything I have to do one day at a time.

In an agonising dream, I had died on the surgeon's table during the first procedure. It had all gone completely wrong, and I was lost. That explained the endless torment and the continued pain, where no matter how many pills and potions were thrown at me, I had no way of escape. Day upon endless day of waking in pain, trudging through it, nothing ends the torture and the agony of living on for another moment. So this is my hell, a place I must endure, and a place I can't escape from. I am already dead and in an underworld of my own making.

When I woke, I knew I had reached my end.

I had reached the point where I couldn't carry the burden of my physical and psychological pain any further. Its weight was too much to bear, and I was ready to draw the final curtain on my life story. I wanted the will to fight it and to be strong enough to continue, but I felt as though all the fight had deserted me like a final rat leaving the sinking ship. There was nothing in the tank, no reserve to draw upon to keep me going, and I was drowning under the heavy load.

A calmness entered me as I realised how easy it would be to take all my pills and potions in one go and slip to the void. An acceptance followed where I absolved myself of any guilt attached to my decision and entered a place of peace. In that peace, the pain continued to rip through my body but seemed to be displaced from my mind, as though it had become a faraway storm that I was viewing rather than being in the middle of. I had separated myself from the agony and felt I could see clearly for the first time in what seemed like an age.

I sat in quiet contemplation, enjoying the feeling of separation from my physical. My mind wandered to places I wanted to visit and people I wanted to see before I left. I must go back and thank the hospital for their help. I must travel to my hometown and say goodbye to lifelong friends. I must travel to my ancestral home in Ireland and make ready to be reunited. Plans formulated in my brain, and I felt renewed with the power of taking charge of what was to come. I had reached a place of rest between life and death. A quiet place where I could connect with the depth of my soul without the torment of pain.

I was ready to go home.

The next few days went by in a bit of a daze. The initial disconnection I had felt from my pain faded, and I was right back in that desperate place. This time each wave of stinging soreness seemed to confirm my decision to leave was the right one. I wrote letters to my family telling them to mourn me as they needed but to understand I was now free to always be with them in a painless way. I collated my finances and made note of account numbers and passwords for the family to access them, and I started to research the pilgrimage to my ancestral home of Ireland.

By the time my next consultants' appointment arrived, I had all but booked my trip and felt ready to take the next steps. Going to the hospital held the same fears as always, but I was much calmer with my resolution that this would be the last time. I sat outside his room and looked at the people in the waiting area. It struck me that we all looked like we were waiting for a bus, silently avoiding eye contact with each other and trying our hardest to ignore the building annoyance at the inevitably delayed appointment time. I wondered how many of them, if any, had got to the point that I had, where the only escape was to end the pain on their own. The sound of my name jolted me out of my daydream, and I staggered to my feet and made my way into his room.

The usual pleasantries were exchanged as he attempted to glean where I was in the process of dealing with my condition. I calmly turned to him and said that I'd had enough. There was silence in the room as he contemplated what I meant by my statement. I smiled at his confusion and continued: 'I can't do this anymore. I can't live with the pain day in and day out, so I've decided not to.' I think it was the calmness in my voice that unnerved him the most. He glanced from me to the nurse and back again but remained in silence as though he were trying to understand what I was saying to him. Realisation dawned on his face as I said, 'I've come today to thank you for everything you've done for me. Keeping me alive in the beginning and all the care from the staff. I would never have got this far without you. But this is my last visit. I won't be coming to see you anymore.'

He knew in that instant what I was telling him. His shoulders dipped, his head went down, and after staring at the floor for a moment, he looked at me and sighed. 'Would it help if I gave you a lifeline? If I check my diary and see when I have a whole day free, will you come and have corrective surgery so we can try and put you back together again? It's still too soon really, and the risks are high, but will you let me try?' Now it was my turn to be silent and digest what he'd said. I'd lived with the pain since coming out of hospital a year and a half ago. It felt like a lifetime, and now, at my lowest ebb, he was willing to try and repair me. I looked up at him and could only nod as tears pricked up in my eyes.

The date was set. On 24th October 2017, I would be taken back into hospital to have corrective surgery. The surgery was explained to me as a compilation of four separate procedures that would be carried out in one. There were no guarantees they would be successful and no guarantees I would make it through alive, but they would try.

The plan was to open my stomach up completely to locate and repair the fistula leak, locate and repair the multitude of hernias, reverse the colostomy providing enough healthy bowel remained, and to pull my stomach muscles back into place by slicing through all the retaining muscles on each side. They would be using pig mesh to hold everything in place.

I listened to their explanation but didn't really feel anything. There was no excitement, no fear, and no worry. I felt an unreal sense of calm that it didn't matter anymore. I was still in the space between life and death and felt if I were meant to die I would, and that would be okay. I still had two months before the surgery and set about a timeline of fitting in my visits back to my hometown and travelling to Ireland.

Going back to my hometown, I made my way around to all the people who had meant something special in my life. I explained about the upcoming surgery, the risks involved, and that I had come back to say goodbye should anything go wrong. I was told that I was strong, that I had a purpose, and still had much to accomplish in the world, so there was no way I wouldn't make it. I smiled, knowing none of it was in my hands anymore, and fate would decide my future.

Then on the 13th October 2017—one day before my birthday—I travelled with a friend over to Ireland on the week Hurricane Ophelia had the same idea. My primary interest in Ireland was to visit the hill of Tara on my birthday and touch the stone of destiny (which my research had shown had links to my ancestry). Luckily, Ophelia didn't make her presence known until the 16th, so she didn't scupper our plans too badly. We took our time and visited many ancient ruins and natural formation while we were there, but the visit to Tara was amazingly special.

We returned back home on the 20th of October, three days before my operation. I knew then I was prepared. I had said goodbye and was ready for anything the fates had in store.

The day arrived. The day I would survive—or not.

I was calm on the journey over to the hospital. My name was called; I entered through the door and made my way to get into a hospital gown. This was it, the time of reckoning, and I felt ready for whatever the day would bring. I was taken to the anaesthetic room and waited while they placed an epidural tube into my spine; I would be fed Fentanyl directly into my spinal cavity to alleviate any post-operative stomach pain. Then, the anaesthetic darkness descended.

The darkness was disturbed when 13 hours later, with my daughter by my side, I woke screaming in pain. The operation had been successful; however, the epidural had not, and I was in incredible pain. It was then I realised I had been so prepared to die I had completely forgotten to prepare myself for the pain of living.

It took a few hours to get the pain under control with medication and for me to comprehend how the surgery had gone. The misshapen mess that had been my stomach seemed quite flat under the new dressing, and I was told the procedure had been a complete success. They would keep me in critical care for a few days to ensure there were no complications, and then I would be discharged to the surgical ward. My consultant came to see me each morning revelling at the wonderful job he had done. I asked how long he felt I would have to remain in hospital. I had been there for five days; he felt another week would be sufficient and I could then go home.

I could feel my upset spike at having to stay and sensed the beginning of a panic attack. The consultant understood my dismay and made a deal with me on the spot. If my scar tissue were dry and showed no sign of problems, he would allow me to go home. I agreed, and his smile was incredibly uplifting, as was his chuckle when he said, 'You win. I will get the paperwork drawn up and see you back in clinic in a month's time.' I was on my way home and had escaped another week of incarceration in the hospital.

After the helplessness I described at the end of chapter one, I believed being released from hospital would serve to alleviate the fearful feelings I had been having. I hadn't realised that instead of calming down, the fears I had would be accompanied by such hopelessness as my physical condition deteriorated. Nightmares and panic attacks followed me from the refuge into my new home, plaguing me daily like constant unwelcome companions.

The little glimmers of hope I had after leaving the refuge and getting my own flat were soon swallowed up by the overwhelming distress I experienced when placed in situations of confrontation or returning to the hospital for appointments. I knew fending for myself would be a challenge with the problems I faced, but nothing prepared me for the physical and mental pain I endured.

The hopeless thoughts swimming through my mind were fed by feelings of despair which became so overwhelming I wanted to give up, to give in to the pain, and have it stop. I lost the ability to separate my physical and mental pain, ending up plummeting further downward in a desperate spiral. I believe the choice of suicide was my way of trying to exercise some control over a situation where helplessness had coupled with the hopeless thoughts I had.

At this point in my journey, I felt sure I would begin the process of healing, regaining some balance now that my physical condition had been repaired. I believed having my body restored would bring some normality to my thought processes and I would bounce back mentally. However, the culmination of these harrowing times fed into my torment and, regardless of my successful corrective surgery, led to a deep sense that I had lost myself inside.

3

AFTERMATH

The months that followed my corrective surgery were a complete roller coaster ride. My physical body had been repaired with wounds that were healing very well. I experienced, and still do, a constant stitch-like pain in the upper left quadrant of my stomach, with an intermittent shooting pain travelling from the left upper to lower part of my abdomen. This pain gets much worse after any physical exertion, and investigation suggests the nerves have begun to grow through the mesh in my stomach and may be knotting up, causing spasms.

My emotional and mental health had been damaged almost to the point of no return. With my physical malady, it felt like my body didn't have time to deal with the depth of my psychological trauma. Now that the physical issue was in hand, my mind began to enter into a whirlpool of dismay and despair. The terrifying nightmares increased in frequency and were accompanied by daytime absences, where I would come to after zoning out, unable to breathe and in great distress. I had spent the best part of a year never leaving my flat, and now, when I wanted to go to a shop, I couldn't even bring myself to get dressed from the stress of it all, let alone actually walk out of my front door. I hadn't expected miracles in my recovery, but I hadn't planned to dive quite so deep down the psychological rabbit hole.

I became convinced the multitude of painkillers I was taking was contributing to my psychological descent. I was informed that, even though my physical pain was much diminished, I couldn't just stop taking them. I would have to wean myself off slowly. In my mind, however, they kept me in a permanent haze where my thoughts were free to take over my rationale. I entered the mindset that to find a base-line balance for myself to begin working my way back from, I would need to get rid of the painkillers. One afternoon, the decision was made. I took off my Fentanyl patch and walked away from Tramadol, Pregabalin, and Oxycodone, never to look back.

The first few months coming off the painkillers were absolute hell. My sleep became much worse where I would lie in bed from 10 p.m. until 2 or 3 a.m. unable to catch and comprehend the thoughts flowing unchecked through my brain. My skin became so itchy that I would stand in the shower and scrub it with a brush to experience a different sensation than the crawling ants that had taken up residence in my dermal layers. Every time I was tempted to take a dose of pain medication, I would check myself by remembering all the reasons to take these potent killers were now gone, and I should be able to cope without them.

I went for an appointment with my nutritionist during this time and had a massive realisation when I was there. We were talking about the residual effect of not eating fibre for so long. I had told her that I couldn't stand in a grocery store and pick up fruit or veg as I would experience a panic attack. As I relayed my dismay, I inadvertently blurted out, 'I want it to stop, I want it all to stop. I expected to be well by now, and I'm not. I still think about taking all my pills to make it go away. It's too much!'

She was visibly shaken by my statement, and in that moment, I realised I still occupied the space between life and death. I again straddled the decision I had made before my corrective surgery and had never really got off the suicide track. I was still lost, not in my physical pain anymore, but by the psychological torture that it had left behind. She insisted I enlist help and suggested I talk with my doctor to see what could be done. I acknowledged the physical pain hadn't killed me, but there was every likelihood at the rate I was falling that the psychological trauma would, and I agreed to go.

Coming away from the appointment I was shaken and distraught at how desperate I still felt about my recovery. I knew I had to become an active participant in my life rather than a passive observer being swept down a destructive path by my psychological health. I had to take charge, I had to find myself, and to reach out in the darkness of my mind to take hold of something tangible and real to begin pulling myself out.

Regardless, and possibly *because* of my experiences in life, I had always been level-headed. I had always been steadfast and strong. I had always felt that I understood myself and my circumstances. That was before I experienced this life-changing trauma. The trauma was significant enough that it lay outside the range of my ability to cope with everyday events. I didn't initially know I was suffering trauma fallout. I knew I wasn't myself anymore. I didn't recognise my instincts or my feelings, and I seemed trapped in a replaying cycle of fear and anxiety which had begun to eat away at my soul.

My doctor was the first one to suggest I was suffering the effects of trauma. He watched me in his consulting room as I shrunk into myself, metaphorically curling up into a little ball of dismay as I failed to express how I was feeling. He wasn't surprised by my dismay, he wasn't shocked by my reactions to life now. He understood my psyche had taken one of the hardest knocks life could throw at it, and I was struggling to cope.

He gave me the label of PTSD and depression and sat back in his chair waiting for it to sink into my skin. I was shaken by his casual acceptance and by the equally casual label he had placed upon me. It was as though he expected it to help me in some way, to ease me in my time of need, but it didn't. I sat with my diagnosis like a sickeningly heavy burden I didn't understand and couldn't comprehend. I felt as though I now wore a badge with PTSD stamped firmly upon it which should explain why I was feeling unable to cope with my life.

The trouble with badges and labels is once you have one, it's like you have been accepted into a club; I was now part of a group of people who are labelled in society for others to understand them better. It's like being put in a box with a handle-with-care stamp and shipped off to the mental health sector. I didn't feel understood, I didn't feel better, and I didn't see how this label could help me.

My doctor suggested I could take medications to help with my sleep and to alleviate the feelings of anxiety that dogged me every day. I explained that I was unhappy putting chemicals into my body and I had come away from all my painkillers for precisely that reason. I didn't want to begin a regime of other pills to cope with my symptoms. I wanted to understand why my symptoms were there so I could start to get my life back on track once more.

I was given the contact details for a group called Talking Therapies in my local area, which put me in touch with a man who specialised in PTSD and depression. There was an allowance of 12 sessions for therapy, which occurred for an hour every week. The sessions were held locally at my doctor's surgery and meant I would have to confront my fears of being in a medical setting every time I attended. I was visibly shaken during our first session. I hadn't slept for days leading up to it, and my shaking distress at being there left me feeling as though I hadn't made any sense during our time together. Each time I went, I would experience intense anxiety leading up to a session as well as in the days that followed. I began to wonder if the extra stress was worth the trouble.

I was desperate to get to the bottom of my PTSD and persevered in the hopes that I would find clarity and relief from my debilitating nightmares. The therapist used Eye Movement Desensitisation and Reprocessing Therapy (EMDR) as a way to have my mind confront the predominant nightmare memory while my eyes tracked his fingers waving in front of my face. Time after time, I was forced to recall the harrowing picture of my abuser's face as he pinned me down, in the hopes my emotional response would lessen. I would sit with the therapist's fingers passing in front of my eyes with the image warping from my abuser's to the anaesthetist's face. My mind was flitting backwards and forwards between my experiences of abuse, and waking up in surgery, as it connected the two incidents of feeling completely powerless. I would leave each session and go home feeling retraumatised by both the attack and my hospitalisation. It left me feeling sad I wasn't able to overcome the terror I still felt.

I found myself feeling sorry for my therapist when week after week the methods he was using weren't helping me. He had warned me at the beginning of our therapy sessions my nightmares would probably increase in the early weeks as we stirred up the memories. I would turn up wishing I could give him positive feedback, but the sessions were taking me longer to get over and leaving me feeling worse throughout the remainder of the week. I was relieved when the sessions came to an end and told that after a short break we could continue the process if I wanted. I declined this kind offer and left wondering if I would ever feel normal again.

CONSCIOUS CONNECTION

I had run out of options when it came to addressing my problems using conventional medical methods. I wasn't willing to take medication, and therapy had begun to feel like I was being freshly abused, leaving me more debilitated than when I started. I didn't recognise the person I had become. From a once competent and capable woman, I seemed to have descended into an insecure, frail, and uncertain being. I began to feel I couldn't break free of the mental chains that had me bound, and I didn't have a sense of self to turn to. I knew I was desperately lost. It felt as though I walked a lonely street without having even myself as a companion, but I couldn't fathom a way to begin finding myself again.

My mental illness spiral had begun during my hospital stay with helpless thoughts fed by intense feelings of fear. Coming away from the hospital and fending for myself had brought hopeless thoughts fed by debilitating feelings of despair. When my physical trauma was repaired, I experienced thoughts of having lost myself fed by incredible feelings of loneliness. These three powerful thoughts, helplessness, hopelessness, and loss of self, represented an enormous circular battle that had begun to rage in my mind. This battle was being fuelled by the powerful feelings of fear, despair, and loneliness I had associated with them. It was impossible to see if I could win the battle as I became completely overwhelmed by my mind and the frightening images it would present to me on a daily basis.

I felt I had become my PTSD and depression. It appeared to control my every moment, awake as well as asleep, and seemed to be the driving force of who I now was. My former self was adrift in the narrative of my PTSD life, and as I dove deeper into the rabbit hole, I felt lost and completely isolated.

Then one day, I was reminded that the person I was hadn't disappeared. In a moment of clarity, I realised I was experiencing PTSD and depression as a maintaining cause. My mind had created a feedback loop to my trauma, and being so caught up in the associated emotional feelings, I was viewing it as still being a reality in my present moment.

I sat in quiet contemplation after another PTSD attack, grasping for some guidance towards feeling better about myself. The usual emotional dregs of upset about the incident began to subside, and I felt a calmness descend upon me. I realised that PTSD is not *who* I am, it is the persistent residue of *where* I have been in my past. As this realisation sank deeper into my soul, I understood I was feeling my distressed thinking to such a degree it was taking me further away from a real sense of self. It was keeping me locked in the cycle of my past and robbing me of being safe in the reality of the present moment. I had unknowingly created a maintaining cause which was feeding my mind untruths. I was clinging on to the emotional expression of the PTSD thoughts as though they were part of me as a person. They were not. I had been getting caught up in them defining me and had lost sight of the real person behind the thoughts.

It was at this moment I made the decision to apply all my understanding of maintaining causes to my situation. I built up a timeline of my journey and could clearly see the steps that had contributed to my self-limiting thoughts and feelings. I acknowledged I had become completely overwhelmed by my distressed thinking and began training my mind to view my story as the adventure my body had taken me on. I looked at the hints it had given me along the way and recognised the subtle markers I had missed while I was so caught up in helpless and hopeless thinking. Thoughts that I couldn't heal, I was a victim, I couldn't cope, I was sinking, and I would never be the same again had become so powerful that I'd failed to see I was still alive and I had survived despite all those self-limiting beliefs.

I began to explore further the limiting thoughts I had bought into and the emotions I had associated with them. As I did, I realised I had chosen to ignore the gentle reminders my body had given me. Throughout the journey, my body had shown me I could heal, I was strong, and I could endure great suffering. I had become so encompassed by what had gone wrong with my health that I was failing to see what had gone right. I had become so stuck in the fearful feelings of despair and loneliness that I had forgotten I had the power to choose how I responded to the stress I experienced.

This shift in thinking opened the pathway to discovering healing answers to the questions that now burned brightly in my mind. How had I allowed my experience to strip me of the ability to choose a healthy response to my stress? Why had I so readily bought into self-limiting emotions that fed the mental burden I had experienced? Where did these self-limiting beliefs originate from and how could I remove them? Unpacking my thinking in this way, I set about eliminating PTSD and depression as the maintaining causes in my story by developing a greater understanding of the breakthrough chapters in section two.

SECTION 2

Breakthrough

If you don't like something change it, if you can't change it change your attitude.

—Maya Angelou

4
WHO ARE WE?

When we feel a complete loss of self during mental illness, what better place to start than with the question—Who am I? Our understanding of this simple question has deep resonating consequences in every aspect of our lives—from how we experience our health and wellbeing to how we experience our importance to the world. It is easy to get caught up in our own stories and wonder who we are within the confusion. First, let's take a look at the broader view and expand our understanding of this question beyond ourselves.

Looking at this topic from a broader perspective helps take us from becoming bogged down by a feeling of having lost our sense of self to a more collective understanding of who we are to begin with. We all share common beliefs of where we originated from, taught to us in our homes and in our schools. These beliefs make up the bedrock of how we view not only ourselves but also our place within society and the world as a whole.

There are two general schools of thought as to our origins. The first is creationism, where the universe and life originated from specific acts of divine creation. This relies particularly upon religious belief systems dating back to scrolls and scriptures that are around 2,000 years old. The second is evolution, which views the origin of life as coming into being via a collection of adaptive biological mutations over time. This theory was proposed in 1859 by Charles Darwin and became the accepted mainstream scientific truth presented in schools and universities throughout the world. While taking my degree in medical anthropology at Durham University, evolution was part of the main first-year curriculum as essential teaching before branching out into a chosen area of expertise.

When we unpack our thoughts around evolutionary theory a little, in layman's terms, there is usually one key phrase people in the room will respond with—survival of the fittest. Somewhere in the back of the room, another voice may pop up to correct this summary by saying, 'It is not the strongest of the species that survives, but the ones most adaptable to change.' Both these quotes have been bandied about in society leaving us with a core belief that struggle, competition, conflict, scarcity, and separation define our origins as a species. Is it any wonder, therefore, when we attempt to define who we are in respect to mental health, our minds subconsciously default to these core beliefs?

We buy into these concepts at a very young age as the fundamental realities of our lives. In our schools, we are taught to compete, to be the best at spelling, math, sports, etc. with competitions to reward the victor. As we move into a working environment, we have to compete with others to get jobs. When we acquire a position, we are then given targets to reach to motivate us to increase our performance further. We are constantly faced with the concept that we have to improve to survive. If we don't achieve a higher standard, we are not good enough, and, therefore, our choices are limited. Our mind accepts these notions, and we create a posture of being powerless in our ability to change them. After all, if struggle and competition are our origins, what can we possibly do during periods of mental distress that will make any difference?

WHO ARE WE?

Neither phrases are mentioned anywhere in Darwin's Origin of Species[2]. For these two phrases to be the most commonly believed concepts in the 160 years since the book was published, a fundamental flaw is revealed in how we perceive information we are given. We allow our minds to be guided by this type of collective belief, and it forms the bottom line of every story we subconsciously tell ourselves. We become conditioned to accept a life of limitation, and this ultimately affects who we are, and how we can heal in times of crisis. The far-reaching consequences of misinterpreting our origins leave us feeling small, insignificant, powerless, and helpless with little ability to take care of ourselves in the presence of change. This is an experience all too familiar to anyone suffering from mental health problems.

There is now a movement to change our thinking about our origins and to rewrite our beliefs with the advent of a new story. Led by Gregg Braden in his book *Human by Design*[3], we are being challenged to accept new scientific thoughts that overthrow our old understanding of evolutionary theory. He does not state Darwin's theory is incorrect; in fact, he believes it explains the adaptation of other species perfectly. He does, however, suggest that our place in the current story of evolution is not supported by evidence. Scientists are still looking for direct links on our evolutionary tree to our hominid ancestors. They infer relationships are believed to exist, but no biological adaptation in the fossil record has been found to link us directly.

Braden examines the evidence of DNA extracted from a Neanderthal infant (who was thought at one time to be our closest relative) discovered in 1987, and points to the study finding no direct descendants to anatomically modern humans. His understanding of these findings led to proposing an entirely new theory. According to our fossil record, human beings of today showed up around 200,000 years ago with 50% larger brains than any of our closest known comparisons. Throughout those 200,000 years, human body proportions have primarily remained the same in cranial size as well as neural network pathways. This new theory proposes we do not fit into the Darwinian framework and is presented as a suggestion that we were born with intentionality. We, as humans, came into existence intentionally, indicating we were created with purpose and more power than our current evolutionary model would have us believe.

You could argue that Braden is attempting to bridge the gap between science and religion, as science can offer no explanation of why modern humans originally came about. Regardless of what we feel about this, he does point to fundamental flaws in our place within the theory of evolution that currently exists. Whatever your belief regarding our origins, it is clear to see our thoughts are guided by the deeply held teachings given to us early in our lives. These beliefs have led us to accept that as a species we are reasonably powerless individuals, and this has translated to how we view and encounter mental health.

We are born into a society that believes we must continue to cope as best we can to carry out our function as part of the collective. Even the most successful people in business experience mental health issues. The pressure to succeed and always be at the top of their game leaves little room for failure. This can be as debilitating for high flyers as it is for those who expect not to succeed. Whether we work or are homemakers, we are supposed to contribute dutifully, or we are viewed as a drain on resources. Mental health issues bear the evolutionary marks of struggle and carry the stigma of not being able to fit in as a functional member of society. This stigma leaves many sufferers unable to speak up about their problems and leads to additional feelings of shame and displacement within the community.

My experiences of helplessness and hopelessness directly correlated to a sense of feeling powerless as a human being. When I reflect back to my place within the school system,

I am reminded that each of my end of year reports carried the same disempowering sentence—*could do better*. Just this comment alone left me with a feeling that I wasn't trying hard enough, wasn't good enough, or capable enough to fit into the system. During my mental illness, I was so caught up in fear, despair, and isolation that I allowed the entrenched evolutionary teachings to dictate my behaviours and responses to the situation I was in. Examining the possibility of our historical origins not necessarily being a story of struggle, scarcity, and competition, elevated my feelings and began to lift the veil of self-limiting thinking.

I realised my responses to the stress I was facing could come from a whole new way of thinking about who I am as a human being. I had lost sight of myself as a daughter, sister, mother, auntie, friend, and partner. I had isolated myself, giving in to feelings of not being worthy of the titles and having nothing to offer. I didn't feel like I fit into my family or friendship circles any longer and had no strength to be a functional member within that community. Changing this thinking alone allowed me to acknowledge the importance of these different roles in my family's life and mine. This left me feeling much more empowered as an individual. I was able to re-evaluate my strength and endurance as I stepped into a deeper understanding of the answer to the question of who I am.

5
PROGRAMMING

We are all using the tools we have been given. We make our way through life encountering different scenarios as we go. Our response is governed by the collective past experiences we have had in the same situation. We are caught in response patterns that are, in large part, under our subconscious rather than our conscious control. The conscious mind represents who we are as unique individuals. It is involved in creative imagination where our wishes, desires, and aspirations are formed. The subconscious mind operates and functions without our consciousness having to pay attention. It controls behaviour via a pre-programmed record-playback mechanism. Even when we experience something we've never come into contact with before, we react instinctively from the pre-programmed part of our brain. This may sound strange because you've never experienced this situation before, so how can your response have come from programming? Let's look at *when* and *how* we are programmed to shed some light on this to develop our understanding.

We begin learning at an early age—scientists believe from before we are even born. While in our mothers' womb, from around midway through the gestation period, we receive chemical signals stimulated by our mothers' response to her environment. If mum has specific music she listens to which leads her to feel calm and happy, her child will respond to the same stimulus by having a pleasant and calming experience. Conversely, if mum is surrounded by a conflict which leads her to feel powerless, upset, and vulnerable, her child will react to the same stimulus by having the same unpleasant response. How mum interprets and responds to her environment is directly translated via the body's chemical messengers to her unborn child.

After we are born, we have five levels of brainwave patterns—delta, theta, alpha, beta, and gamma. The first two years of life are experienced in delta waves. As an adult, delta brainwave patterns arise mostly during deep sleep; however, a newborn produces delta waves when they are awake. During this time, we use our five senses to draw in everything happening around us. We are effectively sponges, soaking up learning through our impressions of the world we inhabit, rather than from the spoken word of others. We download massive amounts of environmental data during this time, which is stored in our subconscious mind for later application.

From age two until around age six or seven, our brains shift into theta brainwave, a hypnotic-type state where imagination contributes to our experience. It is during this period that a child may engage imaginary friends and view an empty teacup as being filled with real liquid in their play. These first impressionable years form the foundation of our understanding of life and represent the most in-depth programming of how we fit into it. Information is adopted, and behaviour is learned through our exposure and observation. This is why children can be taught so quickly and effortlessly without specific guidance.

From age six, we leave the previous hypnotic and highly suggestive frequency behind and enter into alpha brainwave, which brings greater focus, creativity, relaxation, and stress release. This brainwave pattern is perfect for early school years when we begin to apply everything we have already learnt within a wider arena. At this stage in our development, we have already acquired most of our subconscious programming from the preceding six years, and our learning is now based on conscious engagement. Programs are still downloaded to the subconscious parts of our brain, but this occurs more through repetition of tasks over time.

By age twelve, we reach the beta brainwave stage. This stage remains the same throughout our awake adult life, except for those who are able to experience gamma brainwaves. Beta waves predominate and coincide with an introduction to higher school education, where logic and reason are our primary methods of learning and processing information. Beta waves also involve our flight, fright, and freeze response, which encompasses all aspects surrounding our anxiety and stress in our lives.

Gamma brainwave activity is associated with deep meditation and the feeling of being blessed. It is often witnessed in people who are at the top of their game in both mental and physical performance. People with gamma brainwave function experience a feeling of being capable of achieving anything (this is often the case with monks and nuns who have peak concentration). Focussing on compassion, happiness, and love as true expressive emotions in life can immediately produce gamma brainwave activity. Many practitioners around the world explain it as connecting to the rhythm of universal consciousness with a sense of losing oneself in the warmth and oneness.

Sounds perfect, doesn't it? It's almost a little too good to be true. I have no doubt the gamma brainwave state is achievable for many enlightened and happy people. However, most if not all mental illness sufferers are locked in a beta brainwave flight, fight, or freeze response pattern for most of the time. This is why many avenues to freeing people from their stress, anxiety, and depression concentrate on mindfulness and meditation techniques of positive thinking. It is critical to realise, if you have tried these techniques and feel they have failed, that reaching a gamma brainwave state is very difficult if your pre-programming doesn't naturally allow for it.

Up until age six, we are in a hypnotic state of learning where we pick up on everything in our environment. If the programs we receive during this time are positive and nurturing, we download a sense of individual purpose, belonging, and safety. When this is the case, we have a deeply-programmed sense of happiness and love which leads us to easily being able to reach a gamma brainwave experience. Unfortunately, for most of us, this isn't the case, and we receive programs which do not lead to positive outcomes in our lives.

We acquire behaviours and beliefs of prejudices, concerns, worries, and self-deprecating talk from everyone we encounter in our early years. These behaviours are then deposited into our subconscious, forming the central part of our own internal belief system. If mum spent time being disrespected and she allowed this to continue when we were young, the chances are we will experience and accept the same behaviour in our adulthood. If the majority of our childhood is spent being told we are stupid, lazy, and won't amount to anything, then it's safe to say this will eventually become our reality, unless we break through the programming.

It is important to note that mum, dad, and everyone we encounter at the early stages in our lives are, like us, only using the tools they have been given via the programming stage of their own childhoods. The same is true for their parents, and their parents, continuing through the generations. When viewed in this way, it's easier to understand that we may all be responding to situations via programming going back to our ancestors. Looking at this understanding concerning how we experience mental illness, it's possible that our reactions and behaviours to the stresses we have in our lives may not actually be our own. How we perceive stress and worry may be coming from the pre-programmed subconscious portion of our brain over which, up until this point, we had little control.

When I reflect on my adventure into mental illness, I begin to see the possibility of pre-programmed parts of my subconscious coming into play. I had expectations when I was in the hospital that came from generations of belief in the medical profession. I expected to feel better, heal, have my psychological needs met, and when they were not, I spiralled into feelings of insecurity and fear. Members of my family are very stoic in their expression of discomfort. My ordeal had left me feeling vulnerable, so I wasn't able to share with them, and I ended up pushing them away for fear of rejection.

My response to my situation had been riddled with programming, and when I reconciled my new understanding with my consciously-connected mind, I began to see for a large portion of the time I had been running in subconscious mode. I took an inventory of the people who had influenced my early years. I examined what I knew about their behaviours, beliefs, and how they had contributed to my own programming. The simple act of acknowledging this lessened the burden of self-limiting thoughts and emotions I had been carrying. I had felt a massive weight of responsibility over my reactive feelings of fear, despair, and loneliness, and how they were contributing to my mental downfall. The burden became much lighter with a deeper understanding of the tools I had been given through subconscious programming.

Taking this one step further, I began the process of breaking free from my programming, attempting to reach a gamma brainwave state. The process started with the simple step of repeatedly looking at my journey as an adventure rather than a burden. I repeat this throughout the book as a way for my beta brainwaves to accept the information into my subconscious, effectively shifting my conscious connection towards the gamma wave of compassion, love, and happiness.

6

WHO DO WE WANT TO BECOME?

Now we have taken the first steps towards understanding beliefs that have been contributing towards a mental illness framework in our lives, we can begin to move away from that mindset tentatively. Thus far we have looked at how external influences on our patterns of thinking may be contributing to a sense of powerlessness in our lives. Believing as humans we are built into an evolutionary system of struggle, may have added to an understanding that we have little ability to adapt or change. Because we may not realise we are utilising programs given to us at a subconscious level in our childhood, we may have reinforced feelings of helplessness in response to our stress. By acknowledging these concepts, we alter our perceptions of how we experience stress. When we sit with our new understanding for a little while, it begins to alleviate the sense of being personally to blame for our stressful feelings. This is not to say we blame evolutionary theory or the programming we received from others for our problems, but we begin to see patterns of belief in our stories we can now change and learn from.

Looking at early subconscious programming resonated on a deep level with me. I began to wonder if I were living my own life or one mapped out for me in childhood. Were my dreams and aspirations my own, or had they been passed on to me by generations of unfulfilled relatives? These thoughts alone could have taken me on another spiral downwards, but instead, it brought the question that is the topic of this chapter: Who do we want to become? If I have been living a pre-programmed life, now that I am aware of it I can open myself up to choosing who I want to be now. As a sufferer of mental illness, I had constructed a negative reality which was so powerful I felt the only way to overcome it was to end my life. If I am powerful enough to create such a negative reality in which to live, then I am powerful enough to create a different one to move forward with.

We are incredible creators with the power to create the reality of our lives in either a negative or positive direction. Yet, when trying to develop a mindset around who we want to become, often it is the negative that continues to lead the way. Being faced with mental illness, we tend to have a sense of what we *don't* want in our lives rather than what we *do* want. Attempting to create anything for ourselves leaves our minds blank, so at this point, it is pertinent to look elsewhere for guidance. Having looked externally in the previous chapters, now it's time to consider internal mechanisms that contribute to our creative sense of mental health.

New research has identified that we have informative brains in different parts of our body, aside from the one in our heads. When we experience mental illness, we immediately look to how our brain is functioning; however, we are now being guided to an understanding that our heart and our gut also have an impact on our decision making. Both the heart and gut contain neurons which communicate via a continual feedback loop with the brain. Recognising these two mini brains as essential indicators in our mental health is essential to rebalancing our sense of who we can become. We need to get out of our heads and begin getting into our mini brains as a reliable network in helping us trust our life choices once more.

The heart used to be viewed as merely a pump responsible for carrying blood through our system, but recent research by The Institute of Heart Math (IHM)[4] has shown that our hearts have about 40,000 neurons, called sensory neurites, which make up a mini brain. Their pioneering research looks at brain/heart coherence and has shown that the heart sends messages to the brain more frequently than the brain sends messages back. This communication can be accessed if we learn how to align our brain with what our heart is telling us. The signals the heart sends out have a significant effect on brain function by influencing attention, perception, memory, and problem-solving. If we are feeling the effects of excess stress, our heart rhythms will become erratic, which limits our ability to think clearly, remember, learn, reason, and make valid choices.

Our heart intelligence gives us the opportunity to approach a more profound intuition and inner guidance. It can be accessed purely by drawing the attention of our breath to our heart through gently touching the space with our fingers during deep breathing. IHM research has recorded heart rhythm data showing that once attention and breathing are concentrated from the heart centre, and is combined with a sensation of gratitude, the natural rhythm becomes less erratic. It is at this stage that we can trust the messages we receive from our heart/brain coherence as representations of profound truth in our lives. We think with our heads, and we feel with our hearts; if we are able to remember feelings of appreciation, joy, care and love, our heart rhythm becomes more ordered.

Scientists have also studied our gut[5] and highlighted a multitude of neurotransmitters, chemical messengers which carry signals between nerve cells. There are more neurons in our guts than there are in the nervous system. The gut mini brain, much like the heart, communicates with the primary brain more often than the other way around. This influences the expression of our emotions because our equilibrium relies on a balance of the subtle communication between the two. When it comes to making decisions, our gut releases neurotransmitters, serotonin, and dopamine, which are received, processed, and reacted upon by the brain.

Our gut contains important bacteria which influence our health and have actions upon our primary brain. Studies have shown that the bacteria Prevotella affects our emotional and sensory brain regions by reducing hippocampus function, causing us to be more fearful. Conversely, the bacteria Bacteroides causes increased hippocampus activity, leaving us better able to deal with negative emotions. Higher concentrations of Bacteroides also result in stronger problem-solving and information processing brain regions. The way we eat reflects directly on what bacteria reside in the gut. Diets with processed foods that are rich in salt and sugars reduce beneficial bacteria. The key is to eat a diverse diet of fresh ingredients which serve to nurture positive emotions as well as contribute to stronger decision-making abilities.

When we consciously connect our heart centre and our gut with our primary brain, we begin to experience balance from which we are able to trust the signals we receive. Being able to tune into our intuition and follow our instincts plays a crucial role in regulating our mental health. When our primary brain produces thoughts that impact negatively upon our mental health, our other brains are available to set us back on a healthier path. We know in our gut and our heart we can heal and overcome trauma. It's the sense we get that makes us hold on to life rather than giving in. Your instinct was to pick up this book and begin changing your perception of beliefs you hold about your situation. Your deep intuition knows your ability to heal requires a level of personal investment to bring about change. Those two actions alone show that you have an existing mind/heart/gut connection within your body.

Learning to connect all three brains together consciously, led me towards a clearer understanding of who I wanted to become. I moved away from thinking about what I didn't want in my life and found the clarity to define a positive outlook for the future. I want to become the powerful, confident, healthy woman I know I can be, filled with love and understanding not only for myself but also for the people I come into contact with. I want to help others to realise their inherent healing potential, and unlock their wellbeing, so that together we can thrive as human beings.

7
GENETIC MAKE UP

Having begun the path of looking inside for guidance, let's take a step further into our body and explore other beliefs that may have contributed to feeling powerless in our mental health. We have looked at the heart and the gut as additional brain systems, and now we are going beyond the systems to explore the cells that create them. We are incredibly complex as human beings with around fifty trillion cells that make up our body. Science gives us an understanding of this complexity by breaking everything down into its most basic parts through reductionism to learn how the structures function. First though, let's take a brief look at how scientists came to view the body as a purely mechanical organism.

Sir Isaac Newton, a physicist and mathematician, is generally credited with beginning the scientific revolution. He studied the nature of physics, and his understanding of the universe working as a mechanism became the mainstream Newtonian physics still taught in schools today. He viewed the universe as a machine, and even though he acknowledged there was an invisible element, his science concentrated on the mechanical realm of matter. The human body as a biological element was seen as only being affected by physical things, and the concept of mind was separated out under the banner of metaphysics.

Our present-day allopathic system of medicine is based on Newton's principles of studying matter to find causation and responding to disease symptoms with drugs to counteract the effects. Matter is incredibly complex, but the science of reductionism showed that no matter how complicated something is, you can take it apart and study the pieces. When you understand the parts and see how they interact, you can put it back together and understand the effect of cause and reaction on the entire thing.

Microscopic anatomy allowed science to view the organs and tissues of the body and see they were made up of cells. When the cells were taken apart, it was observed they contained carbohydrates, lipids, nucleic acids (DNA and RNA), and proteins. Carbohydrates and lipids provide energy; RNA and DNA carry the genetic hereditary information of the cell with proteins responsible for activating the tasks directed by the genetic information. All these component mechanical parts give us our physical structure and provide for our behaviour, with our genes believed to be governing the fate of each cell. This discovery led scientists to conclude that genes control our biology and, therefore, we are victims of our heredity. If we don't like our characteristics, we can't change the genes as we don't control them. Our biology is not in our control because we are victims of the genetic blueprint we were born with.

With this understanding, we are once more given the impression we are powerless in having any control over our healing. Many people believe genes may be responsible for their mental health as they see other family members have also suffered from struggles with mental illness. With this belief, we buy into the concept that we, as individuals, aren't able to change how we feel as it is written in our genetic code. New research into cell biology and our genetic make-up has begun to reveal we might not be as powerless as we have been led to believe.

Cell biologist, Dr Bruce Lipton, has turned the scientific belief that we are victims of our genetic heritage up-side-down with his research in the field of epigenetics. In contrast to genetics, which views genes as the controlling factor in our biology, epi-(above)-genetics views genes as controlled by signals from outside the cell. His book, *The Biology of Belief*[5], describes in detail how our current understanding of Newtonian physics is effectively keeping us stuck in the old scientific belief that we are powerless. Lipton was funded to carry out stem cell research and discovered something groundbreaking during the process of cell cloning. He observed that genetically identical cells when separated into three different petri dishes, produced different tissue types. Petri dish (a) formed muscle cells, petri dish (b) formed bone cells, and petri dish (c) formed fat cells. He couldn't understand his findings. If every cell was a cloned replica from a mother cell, and if genes were controlling the biology, every cell should have produced the same tissue in each dish. Then, he realised the only variation in his experiment had been the tissue culture medium, the laboratory version of blood, of each petri dish in which the cells were housed.

At this point, Lipton had his eureka moment. He realised the genes themselves were not controlling the cells, but the environment in which they had been placed directed their fate. It was then he understood that we have been given a false scientific belief, and genes *do not* control our biology. This new knowledge led to a new scientific understanding that genes don't actually cause anything. Genes are merely a blueprint activated by proteins, which receive their signals from the environment. Proteins connect to environmental signals via a lock-and-key mechanism on the surface of the cell membrane, which then releases the signal into the cell. Lipton proposes, because genes turn on and off regarding environmental signals, we can create a healthy environment for our cells to live in, and, therefore, change the expression of our genes.

Since Lipton's discoveries, the field of epigenetics has grown quickly in understanding that both environment and individual lifestyle can directly influence epigenetic change. Studies[7] have shown that children born during the 1944-1945 Dutch famine later in life experienced increased rates of coronary heart disease and obesity after maternal exposure to famine, compared to those not exposed. This study examined epigenetic effects resulting from environmental influence in the womb, but it is now understood epigenetic effects can span throughout adulthood as well. What we eat, where we live, who we interact with, when we sleep, how we exercise, and how much stress we experience can all cause chemical modifications around the expression of our genes.

Keeping our genes in a healthy environment can reverse mental illness as well as many of the physical problems we face. The community of our fifty trillion cells are housed in their very own flesh covered petri dish, with the culture medium being our blood. We need to make the best culture medium we possibly can for our cells to thrive and avoid disease. Improved diet and nutrition along with lifestyle changes are essential factors in producing a nourishing environment for our cells. When we experience excess stress, our brain sends out emotional messengers such as adrenalin and cortisol, which alter our blood chemistry and affect the regulatory agents controlling the body.

Studies[8] have shown, between 75%-90% of human diseases are related to the activation of our stress system. Chronic stress releases an overload of chemicals into our bloodstream, which along with suppressing the immune system, also cause chronic inflammation. Inflammation affects our organs and can give rise to headaches, back and neck pain, chest and heart conditions, as well as stomach and digestive problems. Many people suffer conditions such as these in addition to their stress and have looked at them as separate to their mental health. We can now see the connection may have come about through creating an unhealthy environment in which the cells suffered as a result. One of the key determinants in changing this is understanding that we are not powerless when it comes to our biology. We can alter our chemistry at a cellular level and open up a whole new powerful way of viewing not only our mental health but our physical health issues as well.

Acknowledging this new science made me realise I had been creating an environment that wasn't helpful to my cells. Perpetually viewing my mental condition as an ever-decreasing spiral of helplessness and hopelessness had locked me into believing my situation would never change. This type of thinking was releasing chemical messengers into my blood, suppressing my immune system, and causing my cells to resist the ability to heal due to the toxic environment I was creating. I felt my body was letting me down when I experienced problem after problem in the hospital, but I now know it was my own beliefs which contributed to turning off my cells ability to mend.

I had become a victim to the belief of my physical healing being out of my control, and with hindsight, I can see the culture medium I created affected the regulatory agents controlling my healing. Changing my thinking, and acknowledging I can affect my genes by creating a healthier mindset, altered my situation considerably. Believing I have the power within me to create an environment for my cells to thrive was another step towards opening up my mind and my body to its incredible capabilities. I am the creator, I have the power, I can heal my wounds, and live a life of physical and mental health.

8
QUANTUM BODY

Now that we understand the incredible abilities we possess to affect our genetic make-up, let's take the exploration of our capabilities even deeper. If I asked what your body was mostly comprised of, the majority would say water, and according to Newtonian physics, you would be right. Water makes up between 50-75% of our bodies, with 2/3 intracellular, within the cells, and 1/3 extracellular, outside the cells. Water is the primary building block of our cells, it acts as an insulator to regulate internal body temperature, it is needed to metabolise proteins and carbohydrates used as food, it lubricates our joints, works as a shock absorber, flushes waste from the system, works as a solvent, and carries oxygen and nutrients to the cells. Water is crucial to optimising our body as a fully functional organism.

In the previous chapter, we began to incorporate the importance of our minds' influence on the release of chemical transmitters into our system. Stressful thinking releases adrenalin and cortisol into our body, suppressing our immune system and creating a negative blood culture medium for our cells. Japanese researcher Masaru Emoto[9] takes this understanding to a new level with his research on frozen water crystals. In 1994, Emoto began research on the effect positive and negative influences displayed in water after it had been frozen. He and his team conducted experiments using twice-distilled water for hospital usage as a source of purity and exposed the water to positive or negative words, pictures, music, and intention. All instances of positive exposure produced beautiful crystal shapes when frozen, and all instances of negative exposure produced misshapen crystalline pictures.

Dr Emoto conducted the same experiments using toxic water from the polluted Fujiwara Dam, which after an hour-long prayer, displayed geometric crystal shapes found in clean, healthy water. His findings led to a scientific consideration of water as a living consciousness, capable of more than had ever been imagined. This opened up the question—if water is affected by words, intentions, and energies, what does this mean for human beings who are made mostly of water? What kind of imprint are we leaving on our body when our mind concentrates on the negative thinking patterns we experience during mental illness? To understand this phenomenon better, we have to step away from the conventional Newtonian physics of studying matter and incorporate the new scientific energy theory, Quantum Mechanics.

Quantum physics is a theoretical science explaining the nature and behaviour of matter and energy on the atomic and subatomic level. At one point in time, the atom was considered an irreducible unit, and, therefore, the smallest particle of all matter. Its name originated from the meaning[10] *indivisible,* because when the term was first utilised around the 15th century, this was believed to be true. This belief changed in 1897 when physicist JJ Thompson[11] proposed there were electrons—elementary particles consisting of negatively charged energy—within the atom itself. It was at this point that the separation of matter and energy first proposed by Newton came into question, and science began to experience an expansion towards a more inclusive theory.

The word quantum is defined as any of the very small increments or parcels into which many forms of energy are subdivided[12]. From Thompson's observation, Danish physicist Neils Bohr developed the Bohr's Atomic Model. He proposed atoms weren't filled with matter at all but made up of space filled by energy quanta. Much like planets orbiting the sun, within an atom negatively charged electrons orbit a positively charged nucleus, containing combinations of neutrons and protons. The quanta within the atom are in constant movement, vibrating at different frequencies according to the number of electrons present in comparison to the number of protons or neutrons in the nucleus.

Ordinary matter takes its form as a result of colliding electromagnetic forces constructing or destructing between atoms. The electrons, bound by an electromagnetic force to the atomic nuclei, cause this attraction or repulsion. Atoms are, therefore, vortices which give off and absorb energy almost like mini tornados, creating constructive or destructive interference between neighbouring atoms.

Quanta behaves both as a particle, which is matter, and a wave, which is energy; neither of these is believed to be confined by space or time. This phenomenon incorporates Quantum Entanglement and could explain how a mother instinctively knows her child is facing danger in another country; or how the thought of someone close to you results in the phone ringing with them on the other end of the line.

This was the birth of Quantum Theory, which was later built upon by mathematical physicists to give rise to our present understanding known as quantum mechanics. The theory of quantum mechanics is incredibly complex. In its purest form and one that will be sufficient for our understanding, all matter is made up of energy. In terms of our biology, atoms are made up of energy, atoms make up molecules, molecules make up cells, and cells make people. At our most basic microscopic level, we are pure vibrating energy. So, now when we ask the question of what our body is mostly comprised of, the answer in a quantum world is space filled with energy.

Let that sink in for a moment—we are energetic beings in constant vibration in every moment of our lives. We are made of the same energy that makes up all of the matter within the entire universe. We are all part of the powerful universal energy field which gives rise to life.

Our electromagnetic field builds constructive or destructive interference based on the resonance of our vibrating frequency. Our energy field can be easily visualised when we undergo Magnetic Resonance Imaging (MRI) scans, which measure the alignment of the protons within the body. The MRI scan builds a computerised image of the atomic energy field that exists within the various biological organs making up our entire system.

When we look at the discoveries of Masaru Emoto in light of quantum physics, we can begin to understand how energy emitted by positive and negative stimuli can affect the expression of water molecules. The atoms making up water respond to the energy of the stimulus they are given. This can be seen through the crystalline shapes created when water is frozen. Knowing water makes up the majority of our bodily systems, we now know our energy is affected by any stimulus we come into contact with, as well as anything we generate internally.

During mental illness, energy becomes depleted not only mentally but also physically. We struggle to get up, get dressed, clean the house, or go to work because we are tired most of the time. Our mental state leaves us feeling physically unable to cope with everyday demands. As energetic beings, we are caught in the vibration of our lethargy and feel unable to find enough motivation to create a different mindset. Understanding quantum mechanics helps us to see while negative thoughts may begin in our brains, they create vibrations which impact the energetic resonance of the entire body. Acknowledging we are pure vibrating energy can help us to break through destructive thought barriers, overcome debilitating lethargy, and lead us towards more harmonious vibrations.

We can finely tune our energy by applying the techniques utilised by Emoto and his team in their experiments on water. They have proven even the most polluted of rivers can be purified in as little as an hour with positive intention, and so can our bodies. We know one smile can lift the spirits, one kind word can add to a renewed sense of belonging, and for the same reason, we are one thought away from consciously reconnecting with our inherent health and wellbeing. We often get caught up looking externally for the inspiration to motivate our positivity. Understanding we are pure energy gives us the tools we need from within to bring about change.

Let's rest our brains for a moment and breathe in what this chapter has shown us—we are pure energy, and we have the power to resonate with positive thoughts to affect the frequency of our entire body.

If we sit with our positive thought for as little as one hour, we will effectively begin to cleanse ourselves of any polluted energy. This is not to say we can turn around years and, in some cases, what feels like a lifetime, of polluting thoughts in one hour. The journey towards correcting the energy balance and restoring ourselves to health and wellness begins with acknowledging we have the power inside to bring about change in the first instance.

My mother demonstrated the power of quantum entanglement. After a church Sunday service, she saw me across the room, instantly knowing something was wrong. We hadn't had contact for quite a few years, and she had no idea I no longer lived in England. Her visualising me standing in her place of worship happened a few weeks before I was attacked. This showed me regardless of space and time, our entanglement was still strong enough for her to experience my energy.

My journey with mental illness became really affected by a more in-depth understanding that I was pure energy at the core of my being. It was something I had always known deep down, but having so many negative thought processes firing in my brain had taken its toll on my beliefs. My energy had become saturated with fear and doubt I would get better. Much like Emoto's polluted water, I had caused a negative echo which imprinted my whole body leaving me tired and lethargic. Consciously reconnecting with quantum mechanics and the powerful energy residing inside every atom in my body, rekindled my belief that I have the power within me to bring about positive change.

9
INTERCONNECTED WORLD

Quantum theory shows all matter is made out of energy. This means our bodies are made up of the same substance that makes the entire universe. We are energy beings living in an energy universe and through our interconnected nature, we have the power to make direct contact with everything surrounding us. The first level of communication is the vibrations related to our environment, much like a compass reading energy. These vibrations are read and interpreted through either good or bad feelings, which draw us to or away from something. Our feelings are measuring the vibrations around us to determine in which direction it is most favourable to move.

If we think of energy vibrations like ripples in a pond where they converge, they interact with one another. When two energies of the same vibration come together, they are classed as being in harmony. This harmony amplifies the combined energy, causing constructive interference. When two energies come together that aren't in harmony, they are seen as out of phase. This causes the energy to cancel each other out, causing destructive interference. When energies entangle in this way, their vibrations either boost or neutralise the combined energy field.

This process explains what happens when we are caught up in the negative cycle of mental illness. We desperately want to feel better; however, subconscious programming, which is responsible for our negative outlook, produces energy which causes destructive interference. It doesn't matter how good we *want* to feel, if we default to an underlying belief, we are not good enough, and nothing will get better; we are out of phase, which neutralises the good feeling. The same applies to calamitous relationship cycles appearing in our lives. When our energy vibration is caught in a program of being disrespected, we are actually in amplified harmony with those who would disrespect us. This combined energy causes constructive interference, and we experience another unhealthy relationship.

The key to altering the patterns of constructive and destructive interference in our lives comes from working with our internal environment before expecting to see beneficial changes externally. We have already begun this work through the preceding chapters, by acknowledging old beliefs contributing to our powerless feelings. Stepping away from disempowering systems into a deeper understanding of our inherent potential to heal is the first step towards reaching energetic harmony.

We can also utilise universally constant energy vibrations, which are predictable, to influence the energy within our environment. Many health practitioners will advocate taking a walk outside to connect with natural spaces as a way to calm the mind and soothe the soul. What they are saying at a quantum level, is the energy in nature will help us by creating harmonious alignment with our own. A landscape when left to thrive undisturbed displays a perfect balance between the flora and fauna contained within it. A symbiotic relationship exists involving mutual energy interaction between the different organisms living in close physical association. Nature gives us the opportunity to realign with a sense of calmness and balance because at our core we are connecting with the same energy vibration that flows through each of us.

The Moon provides a wonderful example of how powerful our energy connection is within the universe. The gravitational force of the Moon and the Sun pull water in the oceans making them bulge, creating tides. The Moon pulls water towards it creating a high tide, with the corresponding pull on the opposite side creating a low tide. These movements illustrate an undeniable energetic connection between the Moon and the Earth. With our bodies being comprised mainly of water, we are also influenced by this connection. Mystics and pagan practitioners have recognised this connection for years, and capitalise upon it by incorporating the Moon's cyclical phases in their work.

Throughout history, planets in our solar system have been classified as celestial bodies. They are seen to carry symbolic significance and energetic influence according to the Greek and Roman affinities they were given. The two celestial bodies closest to Earth, and, therefore, seen as carrying the greatest energetic influence, are the Sun and the Moon. The Sun—*sol* from ancient Rome, and *Helios* from ancient Greek—is viewed as masculine, providing energetic influences of vitality, individuality, willpower, creative energy, and inspirational action. The Moon—*Luna* from ancient Rome, and *Mene* from Ancient Greek—is viewed as feminine, providing energetic influences of instinctive reaction, unconscious predestination, sensitivity, emotions, imagination, and emotional depth. We know in a quantum world that time and space are irrelevant, and, therefore, all the planets in our solar system have the potential to influence our energy regardless of their distance from us.

Nearly every newspaper carries horoscope readings for their consumers to find out what the week has in store for them. Horoscopes are based on astrology, the belief that the alignment of stars and planets affects every individual's mood, personality, and environment, depending on when they were born. Whether we follow our horoscope or not, it is undeniable that people gain some form of comfort in believing their destiny is written in the stars. When we consider the understanding of how our energy flows in a quantum sense, it is not outside the realm of possibility that we can draw upon planetary energy through our interconnection. When we lie in the sun or take a walk in the moonlight, we can become mindful of their energetic influences and draw upon them to create a harmonious energy balance within ourselves.

There are many universally constant vibrational energies readily available to us. These include, but are not limited to, crystals, colours, smells, and sound. The typical way to connect with these energies is by visiting a licenced practitioner who will offer advice and guidance on how to incorporate them into our lives. When we engage with these energies via an expert, we are drawing a third-party vibration into our situation and giving our power over to someone else. This is not to say the expert won't help us get better, but we enter into a relationship of reliance upon somebody else to tell us what our body needs. The key to finding our own vibrational balance is to try each practice for ourselves and see which resonate deeply, regardless of what the experts say. In this way, our intuition and instinct increase, and we begin to trust our own vibrations to guide us towards health and wellbeing.

Music can have a profound influence on our energy levels, depending on the structure and tempo of the notes within a composition. The melodic movement of relaxation music can calm and loosen the body, as much as an upbeat, fast-paced piece can enliven and raise energy. A powerful way to consciously connect with sound can begin with just one instrument and does not require any artistic ability to gain benefit. Picking up a drum, a Bodhrán, for example, can immediately align our vibration with our heart rhythm. Beating a drum to our heart's rhythm allows us to become calmer as we tap out the beat. Shamans utilise drum beat to induce meditative journeys towards healing. We can experiment with this practice to slow our heart rate to bring about the brain/heart coherence discussed in Chapter 6.

Oils used in aromatherapy can induce feelings of relaxation or excitation, depending upon the desired outcome. Lavender is seen to have relaxing vibrational properties, whereas peppermint provides vibrations which stimulate the brain. We can pick up ready blended oils and incense from any supermarket or scent shop. We will know instantly upon opening the container if the smell is one we like or one we don't. Utilising scent around our home provides a way to connect with the vibrational energy in our personal space consciously, and allows us the ability to mix and match scents for combinations to complement or alter our mood as desired.

Colour is a property of light, a form of vibrational energy used in chromotherapy (colour therapy). Red has the lowest energy, frequency, and vibration, with the longest wavelength; violet has the highest energy, frequency, and vibration, with the shortest wavelength. Colour therapy utilises the visual spectrum of light and colour to affect a person's mood and physical or mental health. The colour blue induces calmness with its opposite being red. Green is seen to relax the emotions, whereas yellow is used to invigorate them. We can experiment with this by wearing different colours to see how the vibrations affect our mood. Incorporating colours we find calming and healing into our homes, can ensure the vibrational effects are more constant. Alternatively, we can create our own colour cards using a pen or paint to affect our feelings in more impermanent ways.

Crystals have long been held as vibrational energies capable of altering our mood to bring us into greater resonance. When we bring a crystal into our electromagnetic field, the stone shifts our energy by transmitting and amplifying the correct frequency to the cells in the body requiring balance. When in contact with a crystal, the vibration of our weaker body will adjust to match that of the stronger body. Crystals are seen as returning our body's energy field to its natural healthy vibrational frequency to bring about healing following the laws of resonance.

There are crystal shops worldwide where we can test out which stone resonates with our vibrational frequency. When we pick up a crystal, we get a sense of movement within ourselves which will feel right for us. The stone we are drawn to will be the one that can provide us with the vibration we require to bring about balance within. Crystals can be carried with us, placed around the house, or worn as jewellery to gain the benefit we require for as long as we need.

As energy beings living in an energy universe, our vibrations interact with everything around us, whether we want them to or not. During times of mental illness, these interactions can draw us to fall into resonance with people and behaviours which aren't beneficial to our health. This leads to patterns of constructive and destructive interference in harmony with our unhealthy vibrational frequency. The few examples above show how we can begin to break the cycle and change the frequencies within us to resonate with our inherent health and wellbeing. These examples are by no means exhaustive, with many others still left to explore. If everything is interconnected, we can access vibrational frequencies far outside the confines of this chapter.

The ability we have to heal ourselves lies in exploring ways to realign our body's vibrational frequency to experience healthy resonance with our external interactions. In doing so, we are better able to trust our internal compass as it guides us through life. We reduce our limitations and open our energy to exploring new pathways of intuition and instinct. These new pathways draw us closer to healing and ultimately to creating a thriving existence.

10

BREATH OF LIFE

When we suffer mental illness, we experience an internal separation of our creative, consciously-connected mind from our pre-programmed subconscious. We fall into destructive patterns of thinking and get caught up in feelings that hold us in this ruinous mindset. When we wake in the morning, and our first thought is an unhappy one, our mood goes down, our anxiety elevates, and we can become caught in a feedback loop for the remainder of the day. The first time it happens we are experiencing a bad day with a hope that tomorrow will be better. When tomorrow brings the same loop, our hope drops a little, and we get caught up in the experience for another day. After a week of waking like this, we have begun to program our subconscious to respond emotionally like second nature. This pattern continues until eventually we lose hope and enter a new reality of going to bed expecting to be unhappy the following day.

The first step to correcting this feedback loop is to take responsibility for the reality we are creating for ourselves. The situation that triggered our stress may well have come from someone or something else, but our continued reaction to the stressor belongs solely to us. Every time we allow stressful thinking to dictate our day, we are breathing life into an unwanted reality. We know we are energetic beings and can resonate with positive or negative vibrations. Creating movement away from our own negative frequency requires breathing life into a different state of mind with the intent to consciously reconnect with healing.

Intention is the key. We must be intent on realistically changing our situation by taking small steps toward consciously creating a different reality. It will be difficult and challenging because we have programmed ourselves to expect to feel unhappy each day. If our first intent is always to feel happy and not be bothered when stressful situations arise, we will be disappointed. This may be our long-term goal, but to achieve it, we have to break the process down into manageable daily steps. Coming away from our programming is possible as long as we make the journey purposeful, meaningful, and sustainable.

When we are stressed, our breathing suffers. In cases of extreme stress, we may forget to breathe completely and find ourselves gasping for air, much like during a panic attack. Regulating our breath takes us from our subconscious brain back to being consciously connected in the moment. The act of being aware of our breath coming in and out of our body purposefully connects us with reality. We take breathing for granted; it happens as a natural part of our system, so we pay little attention to it. Learning to connect with our breath throughout the day consciously is a guaranteed way of staying present, and not allowing our mind to take us to unwanted places.

Look at breathing as the breath of life, a valuable tool in our arsenal against mental illness. It provides a way to check in with our state of mind to be more purposeful throughout the day. This is not like meditation, which can be quite frustrating to anyone who has tried it and failed. Meditation is hard, especially for someone who has suffered trauma and lost the ability to allow thoughts and feelings to disperse naturally and healthily. Every thought can become intrusive in its pathway into our psyche. Frustration comes when we know we should be clearing our mind, but it just won't comply.

My own experience with meditation had set itself up as a need to achieve the ultimate calm stillness I read about in books, but I wasn't getting there. I was forcing myself to concentrate away from intrusive thoughts, and it just wasn't working. It was leaving me feeling frustrated, tired, and a downright failure. Not the desired effect at all. I decided to give myself a break to be more realistic in what I wanted to achieve. I set out to try to feel the quantum energy I knew flowed through me and was sure surrounded me.

I viewed energy as a pulse, a shared heartbeat through the vibrations of everything surrounding me. I wanted to connect with the energy at its most basic level consciously and found myself purposefully breathing through my body in a way that mirrored what I felt around me. As I continued breathing, the energy no longer surrounded me. There was a shift as it actively flowed through me in tune with my breath, like a wonderful rhythmic beat through my entire body. I had reconnected with my conscious mind once more and stepped away from the reality my subconscious had created.

I created six steps to illustrate the specific pathway my breath took through visualisation:

- The in-breath came in through my left hand, my receiving side, and travelled up into my left shoulder.
- The out-breath travelled from my left shoulder down my left side and left leg, deep into the ground, like I was grounding the breath.
- The next in-breath came up deep from the earth, travelled up the same left leg, connected with the base of the spine, and travelled up, out through the top of my head.

- The out-breath came back down through my head, connected with my spine, and travelled deep into the ground again, this time down the right leg.
- The next in-breath came up deep from the earth, travelled up the same right leg, up the right side of my body, and up into the right shoulder.
- The breath travelled out and down my right arm, out through my right hand, my releasing side.

I instantly knew the breath of life was a simple tool which could be utilised any time, any place, anywhere to bring balanced grounding to my life. The principle followed three basic breaths travelling through the body, specifically from left to right according to the sequence given above. The idea is to breathe throughout the entire body in three breaths, from the receiving (left) side through to the releasing (right) side. To feel grounded entirely, I often only need to repeat the breathing sequence three times, this is a three of three, making nine purposeful breaths through the body in total. I sometimes continue the sequence and follow images or words presented to me while I am in this calm space.

As a grounding tool, the breath of life is very powerful. It purposefully places our minds back in the present moment. It can also be used as a tool of exploration, to consciously connect to the universal vibrations explored in chapter 9. We can take a crystal, for example, hold it with both hands, and realign our vibrations using the breath of life to explore the combined energy resonance through our body. When we take a walk outside in nature, if we breathe through our body with the sole purpose of having a connection with the vibrations around us, we can be given some profound understanding. The following insight came to me when doing precisely that.

Trust in your insight and learn from your inner wisdom.
When trials feel overwhelming, turn to your inner self
and amplify the quiet voice.
What you hear you will learn to trust
and grow strong through.
You hold the key. Unlock your being
and trust your voice within.

This breathing technique has now become my go-to stance for any situation where I require some sense of connection with myself and what's around me. When I wake up in the morning, I perform the breath of life to open me up to the possibilities of the day. If I wake with an unhappy feeling, I breathe through my body until the feeling has passed. It gives me the opportunity to connect with the more profound truth that I am a powerful creator, and I can choose to construct my day in a meaningful way. If I feel my energy begin to dip at any time throughout the day, I consciously reconnect with my breath. When I do, I avoid the associated rise in anxiety and am left with the meaningful truth that I am okay again. I perform the breath of life at least twice a day—upon waking and before sleep—regardless of how I am feeling. Getting into this habit programs the subconscious mind to respond with a sustainable reminder to breathe if stressful thinking begins to emerge.

The breath of life technique leaves me feeling whole at the minutest of levels within my body, as well as whole in the larger expanse of the world, universe, and beyond. Using the technique when I come into contact with somebody else, gives me the time and space to access the truth of how I am feeling. This is especially helpful when I am faced with a stressful environment. It provides my mind with a time-out so I can respond in a way that resonates with my needs in the moment. I have found it to be a simple yet potent tool to have in my mental health armoury.

11
OUR GIFTS

Our bodies are amazing systems of regeneration and repair. Key messages come into play when we are hurt or injured; they send signals to our brains to release necessary chemicals which bring about healing. The first message when any disturbance occurs is pain. Pain is the gift the body gives us to indicate something is wrong and requires our attention. We don't enjoy pain, so it may be difficult for us to view it as a gift, but it is one of our most essential warning systems. When pain occurs, it works as an indicator as to the severity of the injury.

If we have a fall and cut our leg, pain receptors immediately send signals to the brain via the nervous system. The message received by the brain will be relative to the severity of the cut. If the cut is deep and severe, the pain message will be severe, leaving us unable to stand. This ensures we do not place weight onto the area to impede the healing action. If the cut is superficial, the pain message is reduced, allowing us to continue walking as healing does not involve being immobilised. Once repair begins, our pain becomes an indicator of which direction our healing is taking. If the pain increases, healing is being impeded in some way; if it reduces, healing is heading in the right direction.

CONSCIOUS CONNECTION

Unfortunately, we do not view the gift of pain as helpful to us, and we tend to medicate ourselves to avoid it. In taking painkillers, we are shutting down our ability to know which direction our healing is taking. Obviously, if our pain is severe, medications are necessary to alleviate the discomfort. However, as a culture, we have become used to medicating our pain. We will take a pill when we are experiencing only slight discomfort. For example, taking pain medications to relieve a headache takes us away from exploring the underlying reasons that caused the pain in the first place. We feel better because of the pain medication, not because we have alleviated the reason for the pain. This action leads to suppressing the gift of pain, as well as ignoring another of our wonderful gifts, the mind.

Our minds are one of the most mysterious and misunderstood gifts in our bodies. The mind is a set of cognitive faculties including consciousness, perception, thinking, judgment, language, and memory. Our minds are divided into two specific areas: the conscious, which is responsible for creative thought; and the subconscious, which is responsible for a pre-programmed action. In our quantum world, the mind is energy in motion, with our conscious and subconscious coming together to make up the reality of our lives. A headache can come about due to our mind becoming overloaded. The build-up of tension in the head is often the result of inflammatory processes released via chemicals messengers during a flight, fright, or freeze response. By medicating this pain, we are failing to explore what may be causing us to become overloaded.

The gift of thought creates mental images, and the gift of conscious connection brings those images of life into a full-blown experience. Mental health is the innate ability to manifest fresh understanding and creative responsiveness in the moment. It comes from a mind essentially living each day from a present, consciously-connected perspective. Mental illness is the inability to manifest these things due to being frozen by our past, and, therefore, fearful of the future. It comes from a mind living each day from a past, subconscious perspective.

We have seen that many of our responses have been planted in our subconscious mind by the programming of others. We have also touched on how repeated negative thinking will eventually form a reality in our lives. Negative thinking becomes a habit, a redundant set of unconscious thoughts, behaviours, and emotions acquired through repetition and stored in the subconscious mind. Our problems are circuits of memories in the brain which become a record of the past. Each traumatic memory comes from the mind and has an emotion which is experienced by the body. The moment we recall the unpleasant memory we feel unhappy, sad, and in pain.

We get caught up in the familiar feelings of our past to create a predictable future. Our bodies get used to our routine, habitual behaviours. When it is time to change, our thinking comes from our subconscious, and we lose our free will to the programs we have in place. We want to be healthy and happy, we want to be free, but the body has another agenda. Long-term memories are created from highly emotional experiences. If we allow our emotional reaction to last for hours or days it becomes a mood, if we continue to hold on to the emotion, it becomes a temperament, and eventually, a trait of our personality.

When we keep recalling a stressful event, we enter into a pattern of survival where our body is pushed into a traumatic reaction. During this reaction, instinctive protection is engaged by releasing chemical messages within our bodies. Every one of our body's systems receives chemical instructions to prepare for critical action, even though we are reliving an event from the past.

During mental illness, we spend around 70% of our lives living in survival and stress. While in this state, we always anticipate the worst-case scenario based upon our past experience.

CONSCIOUS CONNECTION

We select the worst possible outcome for any experience and condition our body into a perpetual state of fear. Our nervous system translates our experience into neurosecretions which allow the body to feel something, rather than feeling numb. The emotions from the experience give the brain and the body a rush of energy which can become addictive. We are not addicted to the memory; our body has become addicted to the chemistry it produces. Our body becomes accustomed to feeding off the energy rush, and this is what makes change feel so uncomfortable.

The familiarity of feeling unhappy is now conditioned chemically in the body, and like any chemical addiction, the body will fight against new thinking to receive the chemical messengers it has become used to. If we try to move towards conscious thoughts of being happy, grateful, capable, and loving towards ourselves, the body fills the mind with doubts that change can be achieved. Subconscious thoughts flood our mind to drown out a conscious connection at realignment: we're not good enough, we can start tomorrow, and we'll never change. The only way to defeat the hold the subconscious has upon our conscious mind is through repetition and reinforcement of a willingness to try.

Our ability to break free from the chemical dependence within our body lies in creating new chemical reactions from different feelings. This is where the gifts of consciousness and thought are powerful allies. Our subconscious would have us believe our past is still very real by returning our thoughts to its programming time after time. It does so because it isn't able to separate our emotion over something that happened in the past into the reality of the present moment. It feeds upon the emotions we are feeling and predicts a future based upon those familiar feelings. The conscious, connected mind exists in the present moment, knows the past no longer exists and realises the future is unknown until it is created.

The best way to predict a new future is to create it through rehearsed action. Our brain doesn't perceive a difference in what we're experiencing and what we're creating. The old Newtonian worldview was built upon cause and effect with us believing we are victims. I am this way because of *that* person or *this* experience; *they* caused the problem and *made* me think and feel this way. However, we know we live in a quantum world in which we are the creator, not the victim. The quantum world is about energy causing an effect, where we are able to generate what we want as soon as we can begin to feel it.

Our conscious mind can create thoughts based on what we know to be true. When we perform the breath of life and sit in full conscious connection with the moment, the past and present cease to exist as there is only now. Understanding in a quantum sense that we really only exist in the present moment is the beginning of unleashing our power of creation. As powerful creators, we are able to teach our body emotionally what the future will feel like ahead of the actual experience. When we practice feeling empowered and healed, we begin to install the hardwires in our brain to look like the event has already occurred. We create the neurochemistry to match the feelings, and stop waiting for something outside to make us feel better on the inside. With repetition, our thinking and feeling changes the outcome of our lives and creates a map to our future.

Our nervous system is involved in the mind's interpretation. The belief we hold in our mind can override the subconscious environmental signal. Belief of love, gratefulness, and compassion enhance vitality and create blood chemistry that endorses health and happiness. Our perception of existing only in the moment leads us to interpret our world in a much more positive light consciously. We move away from a protection response in our lives and move towards fresh understanding and creative responsiveness in the moment.

Our biology creates a reality derived from the picture we hold in our minds. Altering our perception to understand all that really exists is *this* moment creates mental coherence between our beliefs and our reality. This brings internal harmony and leads to constructive interference with environmental signals that enhance our lives and our future.

When I began this process for myself, it was hard initially to get away from the negative programming I had. I set aside time every morning before getting out of bed to ground myself with the breath of life, and then sit consciously connecting to *being* in the moment. I gave myself a target of entering into a consciously connected state of mind, attempting to remain there for 15 minutes. For the first six weeks or so, it would take me a couple of hours of repeatedly trying every time my mind would slip back to subconscious programming. I recognised the feeling instantly because my mood would go down and my anxiety would increase. As soon as I felt this happen, I would open my eyes, grab a glass of water, and begin the process with the breath of life all over again.

After about six weeks, something just clicked. I managed to remain present in conscious connection for a full 15 minutes. I wasn't thinking anything, I wasn't constructing anything, I was just being mindfully present. At the moment my alarm went off, I was immediately glowing inside, and I experienced a feeling of such gratefulness; I couldn't get the grin off my face. The grin has remained, and it feels as though it emanates from within me like a beacon. I have found fresh thinking and wonderful insights come to me when I am being truly present.

If I am negatively affected by my thoughts, I immediately correct myself with a reminder: I am present, and I am the creator of my reality. Over the following months, I realised I was living from the present moment, rather than having to create it actively. The situation of my past is there, but I no longer have my emotions enveloped by it, and my healing since has been phenomenal.

12

UNDERSTANDING INNOCENCE

One of the most challenging aspects of mental illness to overcome is feeling like a victim to our circumstances and the thoughts in our minds. We know neurochemicals can leave the body addicted to the energy rush we receive; however, ego also plays a large part in controlling our responses. Our ego has us hold on to the pain we feel about the situation that led to stress in our lives. It apportions guilt to the guilty in a bid to elevate us away from taking responsibility for our continued connection with the painful experience. When something unfathomable happens to us, we carry the guilt and blame deep within, using it to focus our anger and hate on the external influence. We hold on to the expression of ego and lose sight of the other healing side of our identity—our innocence.

When we feel we have lost our innocence, we carry guilt around subconsciously. It becomes our most significant barrier to awakening from our experience of pain and suffering, yet for most people, it is hard to let go of guilt. Even if we do not feel the guilt ourselves, if we declare others guilty, this is a projection of our own subconscious, as guilt is all about the past. Guilt keeps us in a nightmare of separation, fear, and judgment, whereas embracing innocence awakens us to peace. We have the choice and the power to create peace, but ego keeps us rigid in our fear of who we would be without our suffering and pain. We become afraid of what might happen if we let go of our fears and step into our innocence. The ego may manipulate us, but at our core, we are pure innocence, and when we fully accept that, we are free.

When we look at a baby and watch it grow into a young child, there is an inherent innocence that exists before the ego is formed. This innocence is the deepest part of our existence and reflects who we truly are in our simplistic, beautiful, and organic form. A child is fearless, without a care in the world, filled with love, kindness, generosity, and curiosity. If something causes distress, a child can be easily distracted, and the distress is cast off as though it never existed. True innocence is the capacity to directly experience what is here right now without any demands from the ego to look, act, or feel differently. Children intuitively know how to see through innocent eyes, not look from ego-driven thought.

When we walk with ego in our hearts, we are giving our power over to the person or situation that caused us pain. We want to feel better about our problems, yet we hold onto guilt and blame and live in a world overshadowed by the stressful feelings we cling on to. Perpetuating this state of being means we do not live for ourselves or our health, but we live for the echoes of our pain. Releasing ourselves to our innocence, allows us to choose who we want to be. We are able to live how we want to live, free from the influence of our ego. This heralds in a new chapter of our lives when we are able to view our world through happier, more innocent eyes.

In our willingness to avoid hurt, we close ourselves off to any and all positive experiences in our lives. We fail to see beauty and truth existing in the possibilities that come our way because our hearts are not open to them. This leaves us living an experience of subconscious suffering, unable to see and feel the love of new opportunities. As our innocence becomes buried over time, we enter into patterns of protection. These patterns may have begun with our initial trauma, but they eventually seep into our interaction with every aspect of our lives.

When we recognise repeating patterns and see the price we pay for avoiding vulnerability and hurt, can we really say it serves our healing? We invest so much time and energy in avoidance, but what if we simply opened ourselves up to innocence, avoided nothing, and welcomed all? If we leave the house and take a walk outside, channelling the emotions from our innocence, we will notice how much more beautiful and enjoyable the world can be. We will recognise the deeper truth of what is around us as we are able to feel, see, and know it as a child would. Walking in the reality of our being, with happiness, bliss, gratitude, confidence, acceptance, and love through our innocence relieve us of the weight of anger, hate, worry, doubt, and fear created from our ego.

There is power in innocence that frees us from our ego. The ability to be present in the moment encourages us to live, know joy, create, engage, and love. In the polarities of the mind, living with misery and suffering takes us away from innocence and openness. Our ego weakens us by holding on to pain, whereas our innocence releases pain by making us strong, loving, and creative in our lives. Rediscovering our innocence does not involve being taken advantage of by others. It is not about entering into a position of naivete or delusion. It involves giving ourselves the opportunity to be vulnerable again to discover trust once more. When we enter into an understanding of our innocence, we begin to view the world with the openness and wonder we had as a child. Every opportunity holds the possibility of new meaning, and we give ourselves the beauty of a fresh, clear mind.

Innocence is the capacity of the heart to openly meet whatever is appearing whenever it appears. We see situations truthfully for what they are and embrace the concept of not knowing where they might lead. We step into an unknowing, where we are free from the limitation of ego, and return to our original innocence to create the outcomes we desire. Allowing ourselves to be vulnerable again takes great courage as it leaves us open to being hurt. This is why we bury our innocence beneath the ego's endless worries, doubts, fears, expectations, labels, criticisms, and hate. It takes an enormous amount of energy to avoid feelings of hurt. Huge emotional investment is required to maintain a state of blame, which ironically contributes to our ongoing pain and suffering.

What would the present be like without the imprisoning beliefs of our past? We have already begun to see that our subconscious programming has been dictating our reactions to stress in our lives. We have unknowingly picked up behaviours and beliefs throughout our lives that don't necessarily belong to us. We were not aware of the far-reaching consequences of our negative thinking, and have unwittingly been placing our living cells in a toxic environment. We were ignorant of the mini brains that exist in our heart and our guts, not realising they could provide deeper insight into how to manage our stress. We had never thought of ourselves as boundless vibrating energies which can resonate with the universal frequencies surrounding us. Now that we know these things, we can understand our capabilities and begin to explore them through our innocence.

There is a treasure in the willingness to trust our innocence rather than our mind's protection from hurt. If we are willing to open ourselves and live authentically from a place of innocence, great love and understanding flow through our lives. Love is the teacher of living life in conscious connection with our innocence, where we are able to taste the excitement of every possibility. We move into a deeper state of love for ourselves as well as for others, ultimately releasing us from pain and suffering. If we are willing to surrender to love, we are no longer imprisoned by our thoughts and beliefs. Love is the small innocent voice guiding us towards the truth and teaching us who we really are.

13
GRATITUDE AND FORGIVENESS

Two key aspects of opening our hearts to inherent innocence are gratitude and forgiveness. Without them, we remain caught in a pattern of protection and defence which impedes our healing. The journey to love, acceptance, and strong self-esteem requires courage, strength and faith. It also requires embracing gratitude and forgiveness. A child forgives easily and displays gratitude freely through a sense of wonderment for everything around them. This comes naturally to children as they are living and accepting life at the precise moment of their experience. When we begin practising forgiveness and gratitude, we see and live in the truth of *our* present moment.

Shaking ourselves free of self-imposed restraints from the past enables us to open our hearts and minds to our healing potential. The path of gratitude and forgiveness is much smoother when we learn to stay present in the now and not wander into the past or the future. This exact moment is the only one we really have. It is the only place we have any control and the only place from which we can create. Regrets of the past and fear of the future are our greatest enemies. We must be present, aware, and awake in the moment, or we are not living our lives to the fullest.

Forgiveness is liberating. It frees us from a negative attachment to the person who has hurt us. This is particularly important when it is our own acts we must forgive. There are two sides to forgiveness—forgiving ourselves and forgiving others. Through forgiveness, we can alleviate the feelings of guilt we experience. True forgiveness begins within, with the ability to look objectively at our behaviours. We understand the necessity of taking responsibility for our choices and are often much harder on ourselves than on anyone else. We tend to hold ourselves accountable to a much higher standard. If we are unable to forgive ourselves, we remain in a cycle of guilt and blame which does not release us to forgive others. We cannot give to others what we do not have ourselves. We can't give love if we have self-hate, we can't give joy if we have self-loathing, and we can't forgive others if we haven't forgiven ourselves.

Often we beat ourselves up about a situation we know we contributed to, through words or actions. We might have let our anger or mood overspill to affect people around us. We may have felt powerless and caused pain towards someone else to try to balance the feeling out. We may have pushed people away during times of extreme distress. Whatever the situation, we must recognise and understand we were doing what felt right to us in the moment. We were utilising the only tools we thought we had to get us through the feelings we were experiencing. In acknowledging this, we move towards a sense of being able to forgive ourselves, and we gain the courage to ask for forgiveness from those we have hurt. We have all hurt others some time in our lives, and it can be a powerful lesson to reflect on times we've been forgiven, and what that has meant to us.

Nothing keeps us more grounded in pain than holding on to past behaviour or events. We can't change the past, ours or anyone else's. We can, however, learn from it. By learning to forgive ourselves, we can learn to forgive others more readily.

In cases where we have been hurt deeply by others, we often think forgiving them gives some validation to their behaviour. We are under the misconception we are somehow hurting the other person by holding on to our pain, we are making them pay in some way. This is disempowering and untrue. The act of forgiveness is not about the other person at all, it is about freeing ourselves from our own belief that we must live miserable and damaged lives because of whatever occurred.

Forgiveness isn't about forgetting or reconnecting with the person we are forgiving. When we haven't forgiven someone, we feel anger, resentment, vengefulness, and hurt. These feelings come from the ego holding on to the pain and are not good for our health. Forgiveness is the practice of letting go of pain, moving forward, learning from the experience, and being gentle with ourselves. When we forgive, it is not about validating the act, but letting go of the power the act has in our lives. We move towards healing when we understand holding on to our pain is hurting us more than it hurts anyone else.

We have the choice in every minute we live to move into forgiveness and free ourselves to be joyous, loving, and happy people. This is the power we all have inside of us, no matter what circumstances have occurred in our lives. Our forgiveness does not require the participation of anyone but ourselves. It involves responding positively to transgressions by offering mercy instead of vengeance. Entering into this state is an essential step towards self-love and elevating our energy towards the healing power of innocence. It is a solitary act of self-compassion, solely for freeing our own hearts and minds of unnecessary burdens. Forgiveness doesn't magically make everything better, and it doesn't give us the ability to trust our transgressor. It releases us from the emotional baggage and turmoil we have been carrying in our hearts.

Research[13] has shown that gratitude and forgiveness are distinct character strengths uniquely related to positive psychological processes and well-being. A study of psychology undergraduate students indicated that those who demonstrated forgiveness reported less anger and feelings of loneliness, as well as fewer depressive symptoms. Neuroticism and anger were reduced to the point of non-significance in members who demonstrated forgiveness alongside gratitude. Participants also demonstrated greater acceptance, empathy, and self-compassion, suggesting forgiveness and gratitude are robust indicators of positive mental health outcomes. Focusing on embracing forgiveness, trains the brain for accepting gratitude as a personality trait. Forgiveness liberates us from the cycle of negativity, allowing us to open the gratitude in our hearts to create positive future relationships.

Gratitude is complex, and cannot be separated from forgiveness, although they may not occur simultaneously. It is a positive emotion which must be cultivated with intentional activity to become the foundation for enhanced happiness. Gratitude requires us to examine everything coming into our lives as an opportunity for learning. It involves acknowledging the good things that happen, as well as annoyances, frustrations, pain, anger, disappointment, and sadness. What can the situation teach us to move forward positively? As soon as we view a situation from a place of gratitude, all drama and chaos melt away into acceptance. And, only from a place of acceptance can we hope to come to forgiveness. Gratitude is vital in all things if we are to find the path to true healing.

Practising gratitude is a core strategy for choosing happiness. We are not just talking about saying thank you for a gift, or for someone helping us around the house. Gratitude is an opportunity to be present in the moments of our lives which inspire a sense of wonder and awe. A beautiful sunset, a friend that makes us laugh, or rain on a hot sunny day can all be greeted with a profoundly grateful feeling. We often take these things at face value and rarely single them out for our appreciation. Walking with gratitude means viewing life intentionally as a means of identifying the good in all our experiences, and appreciating the lessons we can take from them. It's an opportunity to grow and be present in our lives, even in the face of challenges and sorrow.

The pathway to gratitude and forgiveness involves making a conscious connection to change how we view our past. Changing our viewpoint requires a commitment to finding the positive lessons our pain can teach us to move on and find fulfilment in our lives. We have to choose to react differently to the pain we experienced and acknowledge the need for change as an essential act of self-love. This choice will engage a lot of emotion as we release ourselves from the mental chains of our past. When we have held on to something so tightly, it comes as a welcome relief to allow ourselves to let it go. We are eliminating our need to hold on to our pain, and in doing so, we release the emotions connected to it. It is essential we allow tears to fall as a necessary form of that release.

Release involves looking at the expectations we had when the painful situation happened. Maybe we expected someone to protect us and they let us down, or for them to keep a promise they broke. We place expectation upon how we believe others should behave. This leads to maintaining unhealthy attachments to the feelings of being let down or not good enough when our expectations are not met. To overcome this, we have to frame a realistic impression of who people really are, and what we can and can't expect from them. We have to remember how stuck we feel when we hold on to unrealistic expectations, and actively release ourselves from them. When we do, we become better able to control our situations through reliance upon our own abilities to fulfil our needs.

It can be helpful in our experience with forgiveness and gratefulness to write a letter expressing our feelings to the person or situation causing us pain. This is not a letter to be sent; it is for us to keep as a reminder of the changes we are making. We can list the ways we were wronged and the many ways those wrongs have affected us. We can write what we wished would have happened. Write about how it has continued to have an impact. And, end it by writing that we've reached a place of forgiveness, why it's good for us, and our heart to do this. After writing the letter, it is powerful to reflect on what we are grateful for in our lives. Picking out the lessons we have learnt and writing them down anchors them in our brains, as well as documenting them so we can reflect upon the riches in our lives.

We may feel it is an impossible task to forgive someone that hurts us so deeply. It might feel as though we are discounting the memory as not important through our forgiveness. This is not the case. The memory is attached to a feeling causing continued pain in our present moment. It is in our best interests to move away from the damaging emotions and towards health and wellbeing. Forgiveness does not take any importance away from the lesson we have learnt. It does not diffuse the memory into non-existence. It alters the painful emotions we have connected to it. We learn to see the situation as something that happened in the past, and, therefore, cannot hurt us in our present moment. We make a conscious connection with a feeling of gratitude that it is over, and we are no longer influenced by the pain and suffering it created.

14
WHO CAN WE BE?

We are powerful creators. We share a limitless connection to the universe through our quantum energy vibrations. When this connection is informed by our repressed memories and emotional behaviours, we are bound to a cycle of reliving the past and carrying it into the future. We experience a sense of disconnection from our health and wellbeing and close ourselves off to the universal energy vibrations helpful to us. In doing so, we create a recurring pattern of pain and suffering so powerful, it echoes through our minds and our bodies. When this connection comes from our conscious mind, we begin to see we hold more potential than we ever dreamed possible. Being consciously connected, we enter into symbiotic alignment with the balancing principles of the universal energy field. This gives us the opportunity to reconnect with our inherent health and wellbeing, eliminating barriers to our healing. In doing so, we create a sturdy platform upon which to build a framework so powerful that we are able to design a thriving future.

We are limitless creators, bound only by the confines of our mind. When we reach into the universal energy field, we touch the infinite possibilities of who we can be. The adventure of our lives up to this point may have caused us to feel weak and disempowered, but the weakness we have felt reflects our strength to endure. It is this endurance within which has pushed us to continue on our journey. When we release ourselves from the confining beliefs we once held and the subconscious programming once in place, there is no limit to what we can achieve. Being present in the moment of now is our most creative place to explore a whole new way of being. We no longer have a past that defines and confines us, and we are free to create the beginning of the rest of our lives.

Once we make the decision to create a whole new way of being, the universal energy around us recognises the shift and creates alignment with our purpose. The words we use, and the images and feelings we attach to them, are crucial to creating the future we desire. Having a blank slate to create from can be a terrifying experience. Like an artist seeking inspiration from a fresh canvas or an author staring at an empty page, it can be overwhelming to know where to begin. We must allow the space between where we are at this moment, and where we want to be in our future to inspire us. Rather than working from the imprint of our previous existence, we are now entering into a creative act for our future selves. We are working with our conscious connection, and imprinting our intent upon the universe.

If we begin with the breath of life, we are grounding our energy with the universe. We resolve to be at one with the energy within and surrounding us, and we become determined to receive wisdom to move forward. From this space, we naturally align our heart and gut mini brains with our mind to bring about a more profound intuition and instinct. We are purposefully entering into a creative state of mind and can begin with a few small steps to measure our effectiveness. The first step is to smile. Smile deeply within yourself, knowing in this moment all past and future falls away, and the process of creating is an exciting and uplifting experience. Consciously connect with the grateful feeling of being fully present, knowing whatever comes to you will be the beginning of designing a new future. Small steps in the beginning lead to longer adventures over time. So, fill yourself up with your smile and awaken to the possibilities coming from this grateful place.

Remain in the moment, allow the feelings of gratitude to fill you up, and see what comes to you. If you are usually unable to leave your bed due to feelings of lethargy, visualise yourself being entirely supported by infinite universal energy, and free from the lethargic feeling. See the possibilities in leaving your bed as you begin your day with purpose. You can choose to do anything with your day. You are free to explore any avenue which will enhance your energetic connection. Feel your body move as it creates meaningful connections between the energy you are building and what you would like to achieve with your day. Notice the sense of accomplishment you experience as you get dressed, brush your hair, and clean your teeth etc. While you are consciously connected to the moment, visualise the steps in the minutest of detail. How does the toothpaste taste? How does your hair look? What colours will you wear? What smells are you noticing? By doing this, you are aligning your energy with the reality of achieving the steps.

Even if we are caught in the cycle of chores, work, or commitments of any kind, beginning our day with purposeful creation brings a more connected and meaningful experience. If we are met with unseen demands, which happen to all of us from time to time, we can reconnect with our inner wisdom actively. We are able to draw upon the intuition in our hearts and the instinct in our guts, knowing they are aligned with the creation of our minds. From this space we respond openly and meet whatever is appearing when it appears through our conscious connection. We are ready for any eventuality and no longer occupy a space of feeling overwhelmed by the unknown. We have learnt to trust our connection and the wisdom it affords us to meet life's challenges as they arise.

Every single day brings the opportunity to begin anew with a creative connection. In fact, we are able to connect with our consciousness every single moment of the day if we need to realign our energy. Universal energy is always there, and our ability to consciously connect it with our own is ever present to us. When we consciously connect on a daily basis, we are able to see the differences in our mindset, energy, health, and wellbeing. These differences are uplifting and keep us pointed in the right direction to bring about long-term sustainable change. Once we are in the practice of consciously connecting every day, we begin to experience the fruits of our labour over a more extended period of time. Our small initial steps build confidence through the positive change happening in our lives, and we begin to see more possibilities for our long-term adventure.

Becoming who we can be begins with a personal determination to move away from who we were. This investment takes time and courage to continue along the adventure of our lives with a reframed mindset. Change is hard, and the unknown can be scary when we have become used to being stuck in our situations. Reading through the chapters in this book may have led to significant insights, which brought about an immediate shift in energy. The possibilities of change might be merely beginning to take root and will lead to flourishing over time. Whichever category we fall into, we must acknowledge the need for change for it to take place. Beginning to adventure forward with small steps makes new conscious connections within the hardwiring of our brains neural network pathways. These pathways create momentum and once connected, they take on more energy to propel us forward in our lives.

Even if we are unsure of who we can be in the long term, creating our reality in the everyday moments of our lives guides us to becoming a healthier version of our former selves. The direction we take may feel unknown to us initially but will become more apparent as we move through each day with purpose. The act of repeatedly creating reality through conscious connection can give our mental creative muscles a much-needed workout. If our muscles aren't worked, they atrophy; using them every day builds up their strength over time. We can be whoever we want to be when we are free of the confines of our subconscious minds. We can create a powerful reality with every breath we take to bring about purposeful, meaningful, and sustainable change.

It's time for a change. It's time to release ourselves from the chains of our past to create a future of self-empowerment. Nobody else can provide us with the tools to be who we want to be. The tools reside within us. We hold the power of potential and the ability to release it into creative reality. We have the strength to continue our adventure under our own terms, free from the influences of the past. Unlocking our potential and acknowledging our strengths enables us to walk fearlessly forward into a thriving future of our own making.

15
WALKING WITH POWER

Living with mental illness involved feeling powerless in our lives. It held us in its grip, like a rat caught in a trap of circumstantial misery and pain. It became our ruler, our dictator, and our fortune teller in an attempt to keep us slave to its bidding. Under its controlling regime, it took us away from ourselves, our friends, and our families. It created fear and dependency through the lies it had us believe about ourselves. It had us perceive its power as all-encompassing and never changing as it fed off our insecurities and worries. It caused us to doubt our healing abilities and had us buy into the controlling thoughts of our subconscious.

We know better now. This is an illusion created to keep us stuck in a never-ending cycle of pain. We can break free from the self-limiting thoughts that have felt so real for so long. We know the truth of who we really are and what we can achieve. Now, we can awaken from the nightmare and see in the bright light of day we are more powerful than our mental illness. We are free to create the future we desire and be whole in our conscious connection with universal energy. It's time to walk with power and live the life we truly deserve. It's time to be a beacon of light for ourselves, as well as a beacon of hope for others, through fresh and powerful understanding.

Our evolution was not by chance. We are not a random act of collective mutations which survived in the face of adversity. We were born with intentionality, and even though we may not know why, it gives us the power to know there is a purpose for each and every one of us. Each of us can live to our highest potential and nurture those we encounter, knowing they are born with purpose too. Working together by talking freely talking about our thoughts and feelings brings the opportunity to change the stigmas within our society. We do not buy into society's construct of struggle and survival, because we understand openness and support are the tools to bring about feelings of safety. We know being gentle with ourselves does not denote weakness; it brings wisdom and displays courage for others to come into a gentler understanding of themselves.

Although our programming is real, we recognise it as something given to us, not something we chose. We understand those who were part of our lives from our earliest childhood were using the tools they had been given in theirs. They passed those tools on to us, unconscious to the effects they created, and the impact they had on our futures. Freeing ourselves from programs that no longer serve us has enabled us to live outside the confines we received. We walk in the power of our own truth and create programs which empower us to help ourselves and others. We view others' behaviours with compassion, knowing they are suffering from subconscious beliefs. Our new-found responses empower others to break free of their own programming to begin experiencing a healthier life.

Our minds are no longer the only informative systems upon which we can rely. Our heart and gut have become reliable indicators in all situations we encounter. Our intuition is aligned with our mind and guides us towards making healthy choices for our future. We trust our instinct to respond appropriately to new stimulus through its comprehensive connection when our mind doubts. Our freedom to make choices now leads us towards healthy situations and healthy people. We are able to see our path more clearly and inspire others to find theirs. We have the confidence to become all we have wanted to be and the foresight to work towards becoming even more. In doing so, we encourage the intuition and instinct in others to achieve this for themselves.

Our genes do not control our biology; they are not turned on or off according to inherited patterns from our parents. They receive their signals from the environment in which they live. The diseases we encountered and the ailments we faced were a direct result of our cells' reaction to the culture medium they were in. By eating whole, unprocessed foods, we are controlling the direction of our health. Through exercise and meditation, we are creating an environment that enhances our vitality and reverses the health problems we run into. Our blood chemistry is a nurturing environment now that our thoughts have turned away from self-limiting programs. We empower our body towards health and wellbeing because we realise *we* are the ones controlling the fate of every cell living within us. Our ability to heal ourselves inspires others to have faith in their own healing power and encourages them to see disease as something they too can overcome.

Our body is not just a collection of mechanical parts coming together as a machine to give structure to matter. We are filled with quantum energy, which animates our atoms through constructive and destructive interference. We are beings of pure energy who resonate at a frequency we can fine tune. As energy beings, we have the power to control every part of our lives, and we direct power to realign with health and wellbeing. We vibrate at a frequency that emanates from us and touches everything we come into contact with. Resonating at our highest vibration, we are able to draw healthy situations towards us and repel those that would damage us.

Through our quantum energy, we are connected to the universal energy field in the most powerful way. We vibrate with a positive frequency which brings a sense of wholeness into our lives. We draw energy from the field and align it with our own to bring about balanced harmony. Our vibrancy flows through us and touches every part of our lives to bring about healing. The energy we give is contagious, causing constructive interference with like-minded souls. Sharing our energy with those who enter our lives, we inspire them to resonate at their own optimal frequency. We make powerful alliances with universal energy, and connect with the field, knowing our contribution brings peace not only to ourselves but also to the planet itself.

Our breath of life has become the focus of our ability to be fully present in the moment. We have entered a still place, free from the past as well as the future, from which we are able to reconnect with our true selves. Our minds receive the wisdom of our body and ground our understanding of the importance of 'now'. We allow the present moment to guide us towards healing and engage in a deeper understanding of who we truly are. Difficult situations have become much easier to face through consciously connecting our responses with our immediate needs. Displaying healthier responses gives others the opportunity to behave differently, inviting them to treat us with the respect we give ourselves.

Our pain, thought, consciousness, and mind have become wonderful gifts to learn from. They are essential indicators of the direction our healing is taking and are drawn upon whenever we experience discomfort. Understanding how the mind works, we are able to see it as a clear sky with clouds of thought passing through. Dark thought clouds no longer form destructive habits as we have detached our subconscious emotion from them. They pass through as the mind clears and we are able to face each day with fresh understanding and creative responsiveness. We have taught our body to become less dependent upon the chemicals of distress and reconditioned our thinking to produce reactions that feed the body wholeness and vitality.

Having entered into our innocence, we now view the world through the fresh eyes of our childlike minds. Every day becomes an exploration of the wonder around us, and we consciously reconnect with the beauty in our lives. We are free of blame and guilt to walk with power, welcoming the unknown as an exciting opportunity. We have opened our hearts to being the authentic seers of our future, rather than looking from a place of our past. Giving love and appreciation for the little things in life, we have opened ourselves up to receiving blessings from others. Our innocence inspires those in our lives to embrace their own and learn from the openness we all share.

By showing forgiveness to ourselves, we have become more forgiving of those who have hurt us in the past. Releasing the feelings of blame has eased the pain within our hearts, leaving us free to experience all that love and acceptance has to offer. Our boundaries have been established, and our understanding has strengthened our resolve. We no longer carry the weight of our grievances and are grateful for the lessons we have learnt. We are now free to move on in our lives from a place of greater understanding and loving acceptance. Our gratitude shines upon anyone near us and encourages them to revaluate their own thinking.

We have reached a level of conscious connection which allows us to breathe new life into our future. We have become the true creators of our own reality and are constructing each day as the start of a new adventure. Shaping ourselves in the image of peace and conscious connection, we move forward with purpose and motivation. Our worries fall away, and we are reconnected with our inherent health and wellbeing through meaningful action. We no longer worry about failure as we know every moment presents the opportunity to begin anew. Living in a place of connected consciousness has improved our relationships with others by being the change we want to see. We are inspirational motivators and powerful advocates of what can be achieved when small steps lead to sustainable journeys of transformation.

We have made the transition from powerless to powerful. We walk with the energy of the universe by our side, safe in the knowledge that we are the creators of the changes we wish to experience. Our liberation from darkness shines a light which illuminates our path towards becoming greater than we ever believed possible. Renewed and refreshed, we are able to use our power to guide others to embrace the light within them.

SECTION 3

Movement

> History, despite its wrenching pain,
> cannot be unlived, but if faced with courage,
> need not be lived again.
>
> —Maya Angelou

16

MY DAILY CHECK-UP

Small steps lead to great adventures over time.

This simple statement helps give me a deeper understanding of what I am able to achieve. It keeps me from setting goals which would be too big, focusing my attention on being grateful for every amazing step I take along the way. With each movement forward, I feel the momentum of my adventure build alongside my energy, and looking back, I am able to see how far I have come.

Freeing myself from limiting beliefs leaves me feeling liberated and motivated to continue into my future with renewed purpose. Acknowledging what had been holding me back was the first step towards freedom, but I needed to form a new reality every day to ensure I kept on top of creating a life consciously connected to thriving health and wellbeing.

Creating the timeline of my mental health in chapters 1 through 3, gave me the ability to reflect upon the steps leading up to the present moment. It showed me what had happened and how it had affected me. It was then essential to build a timeline of how to make sense of it all and move forward from merely surviving to thriving. To facilitate this, I keep a journal which gives me the opportunity to document the adventure I am taking in my recovery. It allows me to turn pain into progress and focus on creating a brighter future, rather than living from a debilitating past.

JOURNALING

Each morning I follow the breath of life practice described in chapter 10. Then, I spend 15 minutes consciously connecting with the present moment described in chapter 11, going on to create what I want for my day according to the practice in chapter 14. My journal lies beside my bed, and I document any feelings and thoughts that come to me through these practices before I get up. I write my creations in as much vivid detail as I can and set the journal aside to begin my day. I return to my journal at the end of the day to record my progress before I go to sleep. If I haven't managed to follow my creation to the letter, I practice forgiveness by understanding tomorrow is another day from which to begin again. I give myself a mental high-five if I have achieved my creation for the day and write how either my failure or achievement felt under the heading gratitude. If I have needed to reconnect with my breathing at any point throughout the day due to stressful situations, I reach deep inside to reflect upon the lessons I need to learn. I look at why I found the situation stressful and what subconscious emotions it brought up for me. I document the situation and/or person I came into contact with under the heading challenges and release it by processing my feelings towards a sense of gratitude. I conclude my day by repeating the breath of life sequence and spend another 15 minutes consciously connecting with the present moment before I fall asleep.

BIOENERGETIC EXERCISE

Every day my body reminds me physically of the trauma I experienced via knotted nerves embedded in the mesh of my stomach after surgery. As a way to combat this problem and in a bid to lessen PTSD, I perform bioenergetic exercises[14]. This is a gentle method of releasing the built-up tension within by allowing the body to shake it out. The exercises fatigue the muscle groups throughout the body, leaving them feeling shaky and unstable. Once this state is achieved, I lay down on my back with my knees bent upwards, plant the soles of my feet on the floor, and allow my body to shake freely. Trauma specialist David Berceli devised this technique in his book *Revolutionary Trauma Release Process*. He has worked successfully with many organisations around the world in the field of trauma release. I use these exercises daily and find that in combination with the other practices my sleep is much improved, and PTSD symptoms have lessened considerably over time.

ME TIME

Each day I set aside time to connect with universal energy consciously. I class this as essential me time when I turn off my phone and my computer to do something that makes me happy to realign my quantum energy. I begin by exploring the interconnection between my heart, gut, and primary brain. I visualise breathing through these places and wait to see what arises for me. In this space, I draw upon the deepest feeling of appreciation I have—usually the joy of my granddaughter—and sit totally immersed with the grateful feeling. I find myself being drawn to different quantum vibrations when I experience this immersed feeling. Sometimes, I will get my drum out and sit quietly, beating out the calm rhythm of my heart. I am drawn towards holding different crystals to explore the feelings I receive as I consciously connect with them. I often see pictures in my mind and explore them through art. I may paint or sketch, connecting with the vibrational energy of colour, or I use clay to create a physical representation of the image in my mind. I also consciously connect with physical creation by potting plants and herbs for the garden or coming up with new ways to bring ingredients together in an interesting recipe idea. Whichever vibration I am drawn to during this me time, I am aware I am investing essential energy and time in my recovery. It provides a wonderful way of acknowledging my need to explore a deeper expression of embracing myself and my life. By creating quality time that belongs just to me, I am honouring that deeper expression. I celebrate these daily explorations by documenting them in my journal.

AWAY FROM THE COMFORT ZONE

Once a week, I purposefully take myself out of my comfort zone to do something to stretch me a little further. In the early days, I didn't feel safe away from my home, only finding comfort being alone in my own space. As I practised creating each day and exploring time for myself, I eventually became more confident to step away from the safety of my house. Instead of ordering groceries online and having them delivered, I planned trips to the local supermarket. I took short walks to the park, sitting on a bench in the sunshine taking in nature around me. As my confidence built, I drove to the seaside and sat watching the waves from my car, consciously connecting with the power of the water. I began finding little coffee shops and would sit practising the breath of life while sipping a cup of Americano, testing my ability to feel comfortable around strangers. Eventually, I re-established connections with people I had pushed away and arranged to meet up with them to extend my social circle once more. With each small step away from my comfort zone, I was able to build confidence and regain a sense of empowerment. I forged a pathway to being comfortable with the once uncomfortable and feeling safe where I had once felt unsafe. The small challenges I set for myself created new behaviours as I followed them through. These behaviours became second nature over time, and before

I knew it, I had rebuilt a life in which I could begin to thrive once more.

PUSHING THE LIMITS

Having achieved success stepping away from my comfort zone, I made the decision to push my limits a little further. I began to create an image of being happy and confident away from my local area. There are many beautiful places to explore in the UK, and I wanted to test myself without the luxury of being able to return to my home. This involved planning an overnight stay at a bed and breakfast hotel in a new area I wanted to explore. I enter the process of being away from home in the same way I create my small daily steps. I visualise packing my bags with the essentials I will need, driving to the place I want to stay, and being checked into a room for the night. I see the excessive beating of my heart as my body's natural expression of excitement at being on an adventure. I assure myself nobody will know I suffer from mental health issues, viewing me as just another tourist. Lastly, I visualise the deep sense of gratitude and appreciation I have for breaking through my fears, returning home refreshed and triumphant after my achievement. These simple steps prepare me to venture out into the unknown, and I gain much more than I believed possible. My first adventure was a liberating experience. I was able to explore a new place, consciously connect with new people, and return home feeling energised. I experienced a renewed sense of belief that regardless of how I felt in the past, I was powerful enough to create a vibrant feeling for my future. I now endeavour to take a trip away from home every month if I am able. It not only allows me to experience new places but also serves to remind me I have the power within to meet new challenges.

When I embarked upon the journey to inherent health and wellbeing I had to acknowledge that it would take time to heal. In the early days, I experienced an average of three or four PTSD night-time episodes a week, with as many day-time panic attacks. These didn't stop overnight, but they did change significantly as I altered my perception of why they were happening. I grasped the self-limiting beliefs that had contributed to being stuck in a mental illness spiral, knowing there would be no quick fix to coming out the other side. Through understanding PTSD and depression as an expression of the adventure my body was taking me on, I was able to reframe my thinking and lessen the intense effect when attacks occurred.

My recovery was a process of slowly incorporating different empowering techniques into everyday life to move forward. The disorientation I felt after an attack began to lessen as I spent time breathing through my body to reconnect myself with the present moment. Every time an attack occurred, I realigned my quantum energy with what I knew to be true. I was remembering something from the past and it could no longer hurt me in the present moment. The more I reassured my mind of this fact, my episodes were easier to deal with, and I bounced back quicker from them. Over time, the intensity of each attack lessened and the space between them grew further apart. This became my gauge for measuring the direction my healing was taking.

Practising conscious connection every day felt as though I had got back into the rhythm of my life. I created a momentum of gratitude and appreciation for each and every moment I experienced. With successful steps forward, I became my own inspiration. I was empowered by my progression and amazed at how much better I felt about myself and life. By focusing on appreciation, gratitude, and understanding, my body regained the tools it required to realign with its healing power naturally.

My life now is a far cry from the disempowered wreck it had once been. The changes I made, and the techniques

I incorporated to sustain those changes, elevated my energy towards vitality and wholeness. Not every day is fantastic and free from worry. I encounter times when my energy will dip, and my anxiety begins to increase. When these times happen, I am now able to view them from a place of understanding that what I am feeling is normal and will pass as long as I stay consciously connected to the present moment. Once I recognise the emotions I am feeling are residual connections to past experiences, I acknowledge it is okay not to feel okay after everything I have been through. The pain serves as a reminder of the incredible strength I have within me to endure, and each time I experience it, I use it as a way to reconnect with that strength.

I now walk with conscious connection, living each moment in innocent awe of what I can achieve. I have become a powerful creator of my own reality and live from a place of awareness where I can alter my thinking in an instant. Small steps have become giant leaps forward when I reflect back through my journal. The timeline of my debilitating past has now been reconciled with an engaging timeline stretching into an exciting future.

I am gentle and loving with myself, and these expressions of self-appreciation shine through me in everything I do. Opportunities present themselves more readily, and with a sense of open acceptance, I am able to grasp them with both hands. Reframing my understanding of mental health empowered my personal journey and has had a positive knock-on effect for those around me. Living from a place of authentic enjoyment has greatly enriched my existing relationships, as well as attracting new like-minded people. I now occupy a place of excitement for what the future holds as I continue along the adventure that is my life.

17
ADVENTURE CALL

Now it's time to hand the power over to you, with a call to action in your own adventure.

The tools to reframe your understanding of mental health have been presented, and the decision to investigate them rests solely in your hands. You have the choice to explore who you really are and embrace the power within you to bring about the changes you want. You can choose to remain bogged down by your situation, or you can choose to move through it to access your inherent health and wellbeing. Regardless of the mental health label you have been given by the medical profession, you have the resources required inside of you to start bringing about change. The first step to living the life you want is having the courage to leave the life you don't want.

One of the strongest deterrents to moving through mental turmoil is fear. Fear of trying and failing. As well as fear of success and moving into unknown territory. Both contribute to a sense of powerlessness, which keeps you frozen in the space you are occupying at this moment. Nobody likes the journey through fear, preferring to bypass it, or get around it in some way to reach the desired destination. Fear has to be overcome, the more you avoid and deny it, the more it becomes an issue. The only way out of fear is to embrace it and move through it. It can feel awful and uncomfortable but being kind to yourself through patience and by giving yourself time, you allow the miracle of who you truly are to rise. Taking the first step forward is always the hardest, but once you do, each subsequent step gets easier and easier.

Building a timeline for yourself is a powerful method of taking your first step. Draw a line on a piece of paper and place a mark at the very centre of the line. This represents where you are today. The space before the mark represents where you have been, and the space after the mark shows where you are heading. Look at the centre mark, and honestly ask yourself what thoughts are going through your mind to keep you locked in mental turmoil. What emotions do these thoughts bring up for you? What feelings are you connecting to them that prevents you from moving forward? What beliefs could be contributing to keeping you powerless to make a change? Do these beliefs come from you or could they be coming from the programming we have discussed in this book? Write these thoughts, emotions, and beliefs next to the mark you have made.

Move to the beginning of your line, make a mark, and ponder on the person you were before you began experiencing mental turmoil. You are concentrating now on the thoughts, feelings, and beliefs you held the last time you felt in your right mind. If you are unable to remember a time when your mental health came from a positive place, try to remember a time when you felt happy, content, and balanced in your life. Repeat the process you used for your present state above and record them along the beginning mark.

Now, move to the end of your line, make a mark, and ask yourself where you would like to be in the future. Concentrate on living a life with thriving mental health and wellbeing in your projected image. What thoughts would be flowing through your mind, what emotions would you be experiencing, and what beliefs would be contributing to this balanced state of being? You can be as experimental with your creative imagination as you like at this stage and think entirely out of the box. The possibilities are endless, so push your creativity to the limit and record your thoughts, emotions, and beliefs along the end mark.

You now have the beginning points on your timeline and can start to fill in the blanks along the way. It is crucial that every reflection back to where you have been is mirrored by a step forward to your future goal. In this way, you remain balanced and aren't dwelling in one place for too long. Your state of mind is going to have a massive effect on whether you are solution orientated during this process. Being as honest as you can possibly be will bring a sense of clarity and make a big difference to the outcome.

The next step is to go back and repeat the process for the situation that led to your mental turmoil. Reflect on the thoughts, feelings, and beliefs you had and convert the experience through your fresh understanding into taking a step forward. Do you need to practice forgiveness? Were your expectations not met? What universal energy can you connect with to bring deeper understanding? In this way, you reframe mental health by consciously connecting with grateful appreciation for the lessons you have learned as you move towards your goal.

Maybe you are able to see the pathway of your forward steps clearly, having moved away from programmed thinking and practised being consciously connected with the present moment. Maybe you require a deeper connection with universal energy to take a forward step and need to explore the various methods we have discussed to realign your vibrational frequency. This is where we all differ, and our adventures will encompass different strategies for forward movement. The timeline is a guidance tool, which gives you the opportunity to incorporate any method of conscious connection that resonates with you. It is a flexible document that ensures moments of insight and clarity become reliable and sustainable as you move forward.

By working on your timeline, you are taking steps to move in the right direction. Each step towards the end mark expands your energy further away from the initial situation that placed your mental health in jeopardy. Every small step forward gets closer and closer until eventually, what once felt like an impossible goal, starts to feel possible. There will come a point where you have filled in the blanks from your past and regained the internal clarity and wisdom to move on from them. Your timeline then becomes a reflective tool for whenever you experience a hiccup in your forward movement. You will be able to see if the thoughts, feelings, and beliefs are something you experienced before, and you have a powerful way to reconnect with how you moved past them.

Your timeline is a transient tool; it is ever-changing as you move towards your goals. Just as your life moves forward, so do the points on your timeline as your accomplishments become realised. You are constantly able to revaluate where you are in the present moment compared to where you would like to be in the future. Growing from strength to strength, you are able to reset your goals as you find your way forward with conscious connection.

You can create the conditions for realisation and insight. There is no doubt your mental health had a terrible impact upon your life, but what we know for sure is despite that, you survived. You made it. Your tenacity to hold on to life shows you have the power to move forward with strength and endurance.

To be real is to feel all of your emotions and understand the reasons behind them. To move forward is to know you are not broken, you don't need fixing, you've had a tough path, and now you're taking charge of your future. Choose to step into your power and become a consciously connected creator.

You are powerful.

You are a creator.

You have choices.

APPENDIX A

CONSCIOUS CONNECTION 5-DAY TIMELINE CHALLENGE

Congratulations! You have invested in creating a thriving future for yourself by reading this book. Now it's time to take your understanding to the next level and apply the knowledge you have gained. It's time to begin your new adventure today.

I want to help you on this adventure. I will give you the support you require as you take your first steps towards a brand new you. Visit SarahWayt.com and sign up for the *free* Conscious Connection 5-day Timeline Challenge. Through carefully crafted videos filled with engaging content and visualisation recordings, I help you identify what is holding you back and how to overcome it. In addition to this wonderful opportunity, you are welcomed as part of the Conscious Connection Movement—Timeline Challenge private Facebook group, a tribe of like-minded souls sharing their journey towards building a thriving future. By coming together and sharing our progress, we collectively reach out to encourage others on their own wonderful adventure.

Free Conscious Connection 5-Day Timeline Challenge SarahWayt.com

APPENDIX B

CONSCIOUS CONNECTION MOVEMENT

Help end the stigma surrounding mental illness. Join the Conscious Connection Movement group on Facebook. If you have an interest in mental health issues, this group shares strategies of action, engagement, comfort, help, and support. Regular, inspiring content is designed to engage members through a multitude of mediums. Uplifting quotes, podcast discussions of common problems, and Facebook Live recordings addressing members' questions all come together in this friendly and engaging community. We aim to consciously connect with mental health at a level accessible to all.

We are building a movement of change. Your engagement and feedback are invaluable to our research within the mental health arena. We hope our endeavours will serve to inform relevant agencies when it comes to making much-needed policy decisions regarding mental health issues. Become a welcome participant of this valuable research by joining our open Facebook group today.

Conscious Connection Movement Open Facebook Group

ACKNOWLEDGEMENTS

I vividly remember the moment I made the decision to write *Conscious Connection*. I had been through so much, and as a researcher, I had documented my adventure along the way to chart my progress. Little scraps of paper littered the coffee table in my lounge alongside my trusty journal where I captured all of my most personal breakthroughs. As I looked up at my father's portrait over the fireplace, his smiling eyes and a mischievous grin brought his distinct voice to my mind—'You have to share this, Sarah.' I've been accustomed to holding conversations with my father in my mind since his passing in 2013, posing questions to him and imagining how he would respond. His message on that afternoon was completely unsolicited but was so clear and felt so right, I knew I had to follow his guidance.

To my Dad, the amazing Peter Roy Alan Conlon—thank you for being a continual guiding light in my life and showing me I have the power inside to inspire others to embrace their future. You instilled the truth in me that with a positive mental attitude and a strong heart, anything is possible.

To my Mum, Gillian Beverley Rayner—you shared a text with me years ago which gave me such encouragement—'I love you so very much and am proud of the way you are working through this. You will win over and come out a stronger person able to help others who are going through the same sort of thing. You will have a true understanding of what they are going through.' Your continued support and the loving embrace of your prayer circle at church have uplifted me so much along my adventure. Thank you all.

To my forever friend, Lynda Upton—sharing the safety of your home and the loving nurture of your open arms when I was faltering, held me in a friendship embrace that will last a lifetime. Having you read the book and give me such powerful feedback spurred me on to believing I have a voice that is valuable to share. Thank you.

To my spiritual cohorts, Kath Ellison and Lorraine Graham—I was honoured to share Conscious Connection with you as my first readers. I am so grateful for the encouragement you have given me along the way. We are forever bound in spirit as well as our love for all things elemental. Thank you for your love, support, and guidance.

To Kary Oberbrunner and the team at Author Academy Elite—without you, *Conscious Connection* would have remained a dusty collection of notes and scribbles in my journal. Sharing your hearts so freely to light the literary way has been an inspiration during times of doubt. Your never-ending support and encouragement along this journey have ignited my soul making a world of difference to my overall adventure. Thank you.

A very special thank you to everyone who has supported my work, research, teaching, speaking, and mentoring. I am always in awe of your courage to turn your passion for holistic health into a vision for a thriving future. Through you, I have learnt so much about myself as well as the interconnected beauty of shared energy.

ABOUT SARAH WAYT

Sarah Wayt is an author, speaker, medical anthropologist, and holistic health practitioner with a 20-year career helping businesses and individuals develop better outcomes for their health. As a passionate advocate for the holistic approach to health and wellbeing, Sarah's early career involved writing research and funding proposals for non-profit groups to move towards a more inclusive holistic model in their organisation. Her client list includes Mental Health North East, Muddy Boots, Women's Health in South Tyneside, Movers and Shakers, and the Workers Education Association, to name but a few.

Sarah has launched the *Conscious Connection—5-day Timeline Challenge* and *Conscious Connection Movement* Facebook groups to engage her readers as a continuation of their understanding. She provides three levels of coaching through her website, offering a basic and extended understanding of *Conscious Connection*, as well as *Train the Trainer*, with coaches becoming qualified to deliver the principles laid out in the book.

Sarah lives in the North East of England. She is blessed with a son, a daughter, and a granddaughter, who all live close by. When she's not working, she loves travelling, painting, drinking tea, and exploring. For more information about Sarah's personal and professional development services, as well as full contact details, visit SarahWayt.com.

BRING SARAH INTO YOUR BUSINESS OR ORGANISATION

AUTHOR. MEDICAL ANTHROPOLOGIST.
COACH. PRACTITIONER.

Sarah understands the importance of having the right speaker to set the stage for your company's mental health outcomes. The messages and training she delivers combine superb content with an authentic approach to engage the target audience. Sarah achieves and exceeds the objective of her clients, making her the top choice for many businesses and non-profit organisations.

CONTACT SARAH TODAY TO BEGIN THE CONVERSATION
SarahWayt.com

ENDNOTES

1. "Maya Angelou Quotes." Quotes.net. STANDS4 LLC, 2018. Web. 1 Aug. 2018. <https://www.quotes.net/quote/42734>
2. Darwin C. The Origin of Species. United States, OUP New York, 1996
3. Braden G. Human by Design. United States, Hay House, Inc. Oct. 2017
4. https://www.heartmath.org/
5. Food Forum; Food and Nutrition Board; Institute of Medicine. Relationships Among the Brain, the Digestive System, and Eating Behavior: Workshop Summary. Washington (DC): National Academies Press (US); 2015 Feb 27. 2, Interaction Between the Brain and the Digestive System. Available from: https://www.ncbi.nlm.nih.gov/books/NBK279994/
6. Lipton B. Biology of Belief. UK Hay House Inc. 2015
7. Painter R.C., Roseboom T.J., Bleker O.P. Prenatal exposure to the Dutch famine and disease in later life: an overview. Reproductive Toxicology 20, 345-52 (2005).
8. Liu Y-Z, Wang Y-X, Jiang C-L. Inflammation: The Common Pathway of Stress-Related Diseases. Frontiers in Human Neuroscience. 2017;11:316. doi:10.3389/fnhum.2017.00316.
9. http://www.masaru-emoto.net/english/water-crystal.html
10. https://www.merriam-webster.com/dictionary/atom

[11] https://www.sciencehistory.org/historical-profile/joseph-john-j-j-thomson
[12] https://www.merriam-webster.com/dictionary/quantum
[13] Breen, William E. et al. "Gratitude and Forgiveness: Convergence and Divergence on Self-Report and Informant Ratings." *Personality and individual differences* 49.8 (2010): 932–937. *PMC*. Web. 16 Aug. 2018.
[14] http://www.traumaprevention.com/wp-content/uploads/2016/01/TRE-TRAINEE-TEMPLATE.pdf

www.ingramcontent.com/pod-product-compliance
Lightning Source LLC
LaVergne TN
LVHW011833060526
838200LV00053B/4001